Museums & Social Issues

A Journal of Reflective Discourse

Volume 7 Number 1 Spring 2012

Eating Together in Our Changing World

Edited by Kris Morrissey and Emily Sparling

LONDON AND NEW YORK

First published 2012 by Left Coast Press, Inc.

Published 2016 by Routledge
2 Park Square, Milton Park, Abingdon, Oxon OX14 4RN
52 Vanderbilt Avenue, New York, NY 10017, USA

Routledge is an imprint of the Taylor & Francis Group, an informa business

Production and Composition by Hannah Jennings Design, Chicago/St. Petersburg.

ISBN 13: 978-1-61132-826-4 (pbk)

Museums & Social Issues

A Journal of Reflective Discourse

Volume 7 Number 1 Spring 2012

Eating Together in Our Changing World

Edited by Kris Morrissey and Emily Sparling

Book Reviews

Program Review

Museums & Social Issues
A Journal of Reflective Discourse

1

Introduction

Emily Sparling

Food, for me, is an internal metric of health. Depending on the menu, you will be able to tell whether or not I am getting outside, connecting with loved ones, or getting enough sleep. When I am happy, I cook. When I am sad, I cook. When I am procrastinating, I cook. Breads, stock, soup, salad, goat—everything is fair game in the kitchen, and no one is safe. You come over for dinner, you assume the role of sous chef. No exceptions.

If someone gives me a recipe, I am crazy enough to believe that I can make it. In my kitchen, there is little room for perfection. Life is messy and so is my cooking. Most meals taste wonderful and on good days look half decent, but they are the product of guesstimations, approximations, and hope. These meals are a collage made up of accumulated bits of culinary wisdom, cultural heritage, and cut greens, all decorating the dining room table canvas.

When we began discussions about this issue's topic, we found ourselves mired in this collage. What is the food movement? Were we talking about new food technologies? Community gardens? Depictions of food by artists? Seed banks? Health? All rooted in food, all relevant, all happening in museums, but what was the heart of the issue? Why are we talking about food? Perhaps it is because when we talk about food, we are talking about our most basic connection to each other and the earth we share.

Food is elemental. Everyone eats—a theme you will hear reiterated throughout this issue. This act forms the nexus between wild lands and the food on our table. It is an integral part of the daily routine of life. For some, meals are something that must be

Museums & Social Issues, Volume 7, Number 1, Spring 2012, pp. 5–11.

done on the way to or from some other more important activity. For others, access to food is a daily struggle consuming much of the family's resources. For still others, meals are an epicurean experience, an event.

Food holds symbolic power. Every major religion practices some form of feasting, fasting, or abstinence from certain foods. Access to particular foods is often socially or economically restricted. Certain seasons and events dictate specific menus.

Food invites interdisciplinary discourse. Physical nourishment does not begin with the contents of the dinner plate, it ends there; it begins with the cultural knowledge of generations informing the way we cultivate and consume; it accounts for the cellular interaction of photosynthesis, relies on the delicate balance of weather patterns, submits to the biology of bugs, and is swayed by civic discourse and public policy regarding appropriate use for land and the deification of one foodstuff over another.

What, how, and why we eat is the subject of intense scrutiny at almost every level of current public conversation. The news is full of stories ranging from the ethics of genetically modified foods to the staggering rise in commodity prices. Weaving together the complex social, economic, and physiological food norms we share provides a rich picture of our cultural milieu.

Acting as a communal kitchen or culinary clearinghouse is not a museum's primary function. Yet, there is a mandate to preserve and sustain communities and their cultural knowledge. Food cultivation and consumption practices are inextricably connected to cultural practices. The values of community, conservation, and stewardship are echoed in innumerable museum mission statements; what happens when we add nourishment?

The family meal functions as an indicator illuminating or perhaps alluding to the physical health of a community, its cultural resilience, environmental health, and overall economic viability. Examining the "family meal" at a natural history museum, chef and author Alice Waters observed the following:

> Fast-food values are pervasive and often appear where they least belong. Recently, for example, I visited a museum of natural history, which celebrates the astonishing diversity of world cultures,

> the beauty of human workmanship, and the wonders of nature. It even houses an impressive collection of artifacts relating to food along with depictions of hunting, foraging, agriculture, food preparation, and the hearth. But in the museum cafeteria, crowds of people queue up in a poorly lit, depressing space as if in a diorama of late twentieth-century life, surrounded by the unmistakable steam-table smell of precooked, portion-controlled food. In this marvelous museum, surrounded on all sides by splendid exhibits that celebrate the complexity of life and the diversity of human achievement, people appear to have stopped thinking when it comes to their very own everyday experience. People appear to be oblivious to the fact that the cafeteria represents the antithesis of the values celebrated in the museum. (2008, p. 5)

Museums have been challenged with a daunting task by internal and external stakeholders: address issues of cultural *and* environmental sustainability as well as physical *and* environmental health. The discourse within the food movement seems to have found a way to marry these issues. Though opportunities to connect with the food movement exist, there is a paucity of models available for understanding how museums can interface with this movement. In the following pages we will explore some emerging models in greater depth.

The mission of this issue is to explore the intersection of the food movement and museum practice. We asked ourselves, where do we find overlap? Are there models arising from the food movement that could have relevancy at the museum? The articles in this issue provide glimpses into the vast, nebulous food movement in America and around the world. Each program represented differs according to the specific focus and location of its parent institution, but the unifying principle is that food can provide visitors an access point to your institution, regardless of your geographical locale or discipline—be it science, art, or natural history.

The journal begins with "Because Food Can Change the World" by Elizabeth Merritt of the Center for the Future of Museums (CMF). This article is a continuation of the conversations begun last October during the first-ever food symposium, Feeding the Spirit, sponsored by the CFM. Housed in the beautiful Phipps

Conservatory & Botanical Gardens and hosted by the Phipps staff (see the cover of this issue for a glimpse of the delicious food we enjoyed), the symposium brought together food service professionals, major gifts officers, farmers, culinary historians, educators, and chefs, among many others. Sharing the table with these diverse dinner guests invited great conversation. We discussed ways to carry the mission of an institution from the exhibit hall to the dining hall and back. Merritt's piece provides a broad survey of current trends within the field, supplemented by concrete, practical steps for museums to consider when thinking about integrating food into programming.

These steps become even more valuable in light of the partnership between the Institute of Museum and Library Services and First Lady Michelle Obama's Let's Move initiative. Viewed in conjunction with the piece by Alice Kamps et al. from the National Archives—an unlikely source for food programming inspiration—we see the extent to which any institution can incorporate food. By combining the tactile (food) with the textual (recipes from the archives), the National Archives invited a new audience to engage with their collections, fostered partnerships with chefs, and opened a restaurant!

One characteristic of the emerging food movement discussed at the CFM symposium was the repairing of relationships between consumers and farmers. Erika Allen's thought piece, "The Good Food Story," examines the history of those relationships. She unpacks the correlation of food sovereignty—the agency a community has in its food system—to community well being. Growing Power, the organization founded by Allen's father, is working to reclaim urban spaces for farms and redeem the troubled legacy of African Americans in agriculture.

"Cooking Our Native Landscapes, Eating Our Indigenous Cultures" by Enrique Salmon reveals the ways identity, community, health, and family are bound in the family meal. His article marries the sensuous elements of food—the tastes, smells, sounds, and textures—with the cultural—feasting, community gathering, celebration, and support. Eating is an intimate act inextricably linked to memory; bringing the meal into the museum invites visitors closer than perhaps we have ever been able to get them to come.

The two book reviews in this issue reflect and reinforce this thesis. A.V. Crofts reviewed Maman's Homesick Pie: A Persian Heart in an American Kitchen. Of this memoir Crofts observed, "[R]ecipes provide ballast to those forced to reinvent themselves, as exiles must." Beck Tench reviewed Everlasting Meal: Cooking with Economy and Grace. She went beyond her role as reviewer to include a simple salad recipe of her own, adding to the connecting narrative of food in "Eating Together."

Lisa Roberts reviews the work of the Jane Addams Hull-House whose constellation of food programs includes a seed bank, "a way to get many more varieties of seeds—especially those well suited to local growing conditions—into the hands of gardeners than might ordinarily be available at the average nursery. It is a way of conserving the remaining diversity of the planet's seed stock." The social work of the Hull-House is enacted through its culinary outreach, similar to projects such as the Science Museum of Minnesota's (SMM) program with Native American youth, Tending Traditions, which "is teaching culturally relevant planting and harvesting techniques" (SMM, 2012).

Another characteristic of the food movement is its strange vocabulary. Words and phrases like cottage food industry, GMO, farm-to-table, CAFO, raw, pro-biotic, gluten free, vegan, grass-fed mingle with the old standbys butter, sugar, eggs (Cage-free? Nested? Pastured?) and flour. How do eaters navigate this linguistic quagmire? The anecdotal semantic lines in the sand—a good plant is a vegetable, a bad plant is a factory—have not always served the best interests of the public. Food researchers Mary Nucci and William Hallman invite museums to unpack "food technologies" in service of increasing science literacy in communities. The echo of empowering consumers and communities to make informed decisions runs throughout these articles.

In the decidedly low-tech Pickle Project model, author Linda Norris writes, "food conversations can be powerful catalysts towards civic engagement." Norris's piece addresses a core tenet uniting this collection of articles—the dinner table can provide a platform for conversations that can change the world.

Reporting from the Cape Cod Children's Museum, Lori Lieberman details the Little Sprouts program connecting kids to a neighborhood farm. Her observations of the 3- to 10-year-old kids involved in the program resonate with the findings of Dorothy Blair (2009). Blair's 2009 aggregate of 19 mixed-method quantitative and qualitative studies on garden practices across the United States is one of the most comprehensive studies of garden programming to date. From the combined qualitative data set she identified reoccurring themes of "heightened motivation and enthusiasm, improved sense of self, teamwork, community, and parental involvement" (p. 35). The study also explored the interdisciplinary nature of gardens, concluding, "[G]ardens provide another kind of lesson, one about human interaction with the natural world" (p. 18). On the ground and in the academy, the transformation of kids in the garden is being observed.

At the end of this issue we find ourselves back at the collage. We had such an overwhelming response from programs across the globe that we decided to include a sampling of short stories of programs near and far. The "small plate—big ideas" Tapas section starts with a bison roast and ends with dinner in Cyprus.

Changing food norms within society are the impetus for this issue. Food habits affect everyone and every sector of society, and thus, by extension, every museum. Food is more than a topic that allows us to explore important issues; it is a way of being in the world. So pull up a chair; let's sit at the table and enjoy the feast before us.

References

Blair, D. (2009). The child in the garden: An evaluative review of the benefits of school gardening. *The Journal of Environmental Education,* 40(2), 15–38.

Chez Panisse Foundation. (2008). *Ten years of education at the edible schoolyard; Cultivating a new generation.* Berkeley.

Science Museum of Minnesota. (2012). Anthropology. Retrieved from www.smm.org/anthropology/ethnobotany/

About the author

Emily Sparling has an MA in Museology from the University of Washington and is a freelance writer and consultant. Her research focuses on whole-person learning and edible education. Together with her husband, she ranches and raises vegetables in the foothills of the Sierra Nevada Mountains, but this fall will call the Shenandoah River Valley home.

Because Food Can Change the World

Elizabeth Merritt

Abstract
In 2011, the American Alliance of Museums launched an exploratory expedition into the world of food, led by AAM's Center for the Future of Museums. Many museums enthusiastically signed on for the trek. Others regarded the invitation with bafflement and asked, in effect, "Why food?" This article shares examples of ways that museums are engaging with their communities and their own operations around food and food issues, particularly around the themes of education, food services, and food as connector. The article shares a number of lessons and sage advice from museums across the country exploring the place of food in advancing the mission of museums.

About the author
Elizabeth Merritt is founding director of AAM's Center for the Future of Museums (CFM). Prior to joining AAM in 1999 she had 15 years of experience in museums, primarily in collections care and research. Her books include *National Standards and Best Practices for U.S. Museums* and the *AAM Guide to Collections Planning*. She blogs for CFM at futureofmuseums.blogspot.com and tweets as @futureofmuseums.

Museums & Social Issues, Volume 7, Number 1, Spring 2012, pp. 13–21.

The Center for the Future of Museums (CFM) was founded to help museums track and respond to the trends that will shape their communities in coming decades. And food, in so many ways, is embedded in the changes and challenges that face society. America is immersed in a reexamination of its relationship to food. The collective issues of sustainability—human and environmental health, food equity, and social cohesion—pose some of the greatest challenges facing the United States in coming decades. There is a growing sentiment that our current systems for growing, distributing, and eating food are unsustainable, inflicting damage on our health and our environment.

The experience of growing food reconnects us to nature and fosters thoughtful awareness about what we eat. Preparing food helps us to share traditions and culture. And food influences attendance. Research on participation in the arts shows that while people are becoming less likely to partake of "high culture" (museums, classical music concerts, theater, dance), they increasingly attend multi-faceted cultural events that include food in the mix. Young people say an important aspect of a welcoming public environment is the ability to eat and drink with friends.

AAM's *Feeding the Spirit* initiative encourages museums to respond to these challenges by helping their communities explore our collective values about food, our bodies, our environment, and society. It is a way to unify the field around key messages about food critical to transforming the health of the country and encourage museums to integrate these messages into their exhibits, programs, and operations.

As we surveyed the myriad ways that museums are engaging with their communities and their own operations around food and food issues, three major areas of focus emerged.

Education

Many communities in America lack access to fresh, healthy food; school lunch programs struggle with barriers that make it difficult to promote healthy eating; attitudes towards food choices are changing incrementally while behavior lags behind; the obesity epidemic may be slowing, but its health effects will be felt for decades through increased rates of heart disease, diabetes, and other weight-related ailments. There is a growing sentiment that our current systems for growing, distributing, and eating food are unsustainable, inflicting damage on our health and our environment. Many museums are helping their communities tackle these issues by promoting "food literacy" through exhibits, programs, partnerships, and business ventures.

Food Services

According to AAM's *2009 Museum Financial Information,* nearly one-third of museums have on-site food services, and these can occupy significant footprints in the building. Rarely do museums treat these important sites of visitor engagement as integral to mission delivery. However, we find that some museums that are committed to promoting health, nutrition, and sustainability are also embedding these values in the operations of their restaurants, cafeterias, and catering. Museums are adding interpretation and messaging about nutrition and health into their food services. They are considering the environmental and economic impact of what kind of food they buy and from whom. Some are deliberately taking a lower profit on the food operation, or assuming greater risk, to ensure that the messages embedded in the food they serve are consistent with their mission and values.

Food as Connector

Museums are struggling to diversify their audiences as the United States undergoes gradual but dramatic demographic transformation. According to research from Reach Advisors, nine out of ten core visitors (those who engage deeply with the museum) are Caucasian. Within 25 years, America will be "majority-minority" with no one racial or ethnic group predominating. In many major metropolitan areas and five states this future is already here. How can museums become welcome and familiar destinations to people from groups that have, historically, no tradition of museum-going? Food may provide one bridge. Over and over again, museum staff have told us that "food is the universal communicator."

Food can play a key role in fostering relationships, building new audiences and creating financial sustainability for museums. As communities increasingly self-sort by politics, race, culture, and income, food is one of the deeply human ways we come together and explore commonalities. Preparing food helps us to share traditions and culture.

And museums are heeding the fact that food strongly influences where and how we spend our time. For example, recent research by Reach Advisors (unpublished) of cultural consumers in the Atlanta metro area found that over half enjoyed cooking or baking at home in their leisure time, or considered eating authentic or ethnic foods from the past as their favorite way of experiencing history. These "foodies" seek out participatory, food-related experiences at museums, which is a significant marketing opportunity. The Wyck Historic House & Garden in Philadelphia developed a farm that grows food for a weekly on-site farmers market and serves as an interactive, outdoor classroom for local children and adults, thus perpetuating Wyck's 300-year-old agricultural traditions. The Home Farm and related programs have caused Wyck's audience to more than *double* in the three years since the farm began.

What about Mission?

Putting aside the issue of how museums run their food services, the most common reason I hear given for not addressing food or food issues is "it isn't related to our mission." The wildly creative efforts of museums of all types involved in *Feeding the Spirit* suggest that this response may reflect a lack of imagination. We see history museums interpreting traditional foodways, and historic sites reviving their period-appropriate gardens or demonstrating historic cooking. Art museums explore the history of our attitudes towards weight and beauty, the aesthetics of food, cooking, and dining. Natural history museums delve into our evolutionary relationship with food, and science museums unpick the complex factors underlying the current obesity epidemic. So while addressing food or not is a choice, it is not a choice constrained by a museum's mission.

Some visionary museums consider their mission as a starting point that can grow to encompass the general public good. Dorothy Kosinski, director of The Phillips Collection in Washington, DC, notes "for me, the future of museums has a lot to do with supporting an overall sense of well-being for our visitors and community. In our founder Duncan Phillips's words, The Phillips Collection is about a 'joy-giving, life-enhancing' experience with art and, I believe, that extends off the walls to the health and wellness of the people within them" (Kosinksi, 2011).

Self-preservation

Mission aside, sound business sense suggests that it is in museums' best interests to help address the food-related challenges facing our country. Nearly one-third of adults and 17% of children in the United States are overweight or obese. This is leading to an increase in obesity-related illnesses and disabilities such as type 2 diabetes, cardiovascular disease, hypertension, stroke, and certain forms of cancer. In 2008, obesity-related health care cost the United States $147 billion (Finkelstein et. al., 2009). If current trends continue, by 2018 more than 40% of adults in the United States will be obese, and spending on the epidemic will more than double to $344 billion (United Health Foundation, 2009).

This obesity epidemic is a drain on the economic health of our communities. And it may rob museums of their visitors by fostering a population that will find it difficult to visit or enjoy museums—a fact that has not gone unnoticed. The B.B. King Museum and Delta Interpretive Center, in Indianola, Mississippi, created a seven-week summer day camp for children ages 6–15—The Art of Living Smart—in part because Mississippi is the most obese state in the nation, with 44% of its children obese or overweight. Such projects can be both altruistic *and* self-interested.

Lessons Learned

Having spent over a year and a half seeking examples of museums working with food and on food issues, I heard a lot about what does or does not work, and what museums can do to increase their chances of success. Here is a quick overview of some of that sage advice.

Partnerships are crucial. When it comes to issues of food, and health, museums rarely have all the expertise and resources they need in-house. The Yale Peabody Museum of Natural History drew on the research and connections of the university's Rudd Center for Food Policy and Obesity and the School of Health's Community Alliance for Research and Engagement. Together with the knowledge of their own anthropology staff, this gave the museum access to the depth of knowledge they needed to tackle the complicated story of how and why we as a people are gaining weight. Woodlawn, a site run by the National Trust for Historic preservation, was originally a working farm that formed part of George Washington's Mount Vernon estate. To return some of the grounds to cultivation (undoing the historically inaccurate 1950s era interpretation of the grounds as boxwood-bordered parterres) Woodlawn teamed up with restaurateur and entrepreneur Michael Babin. Babin needed land to pursue his goals of raising local, organic food for his Neighborhood Restaurant Group and creating a sustainable food culture in the DC area. Together, they formed the Arcadia Center for Sustainable Food and Agriculture, which provides experiential learning for students, linking local farmers to a workable distribution network, fielding a mobile food market to DC's food deserts, and working to get healthy sustainable food into the local school system. And (not incidentally) they created a whole new audience and fan base for Woodlawn.

Plan for the long haul. Many of the meaningful changes a museum can make in how it addresses food involve investment in infrastructure. The Phipps Conservatory and Botanical Gardens in Pittsburgh, Pennsylvania, has a long term facilities plan for integrating equipment that will help its transition to truly green food service: adding a commercial grade dishwasher, for example, so they can eliminate the use of disposable cutlery. Having converted a portion of its ground to a working garden for the exhibit "The White House Children's Garden" in 2011, The Stearns History

Museum in St. Cloud, Minnesota, now replants the site to interpret a rotating crop of relevant themes: a Native American garden, a WWII-era victory garden. The New York Botanical Garden (NYBG) built a kitchen stage in front of their landmark Enid A. Haupt Conservatory to feature cooking demonstrations that help adults make healthy choices at home and inspire them to grow and prepare meals from fresh, garden-grown ingredients. In the end, these investments can pay back. The Phipps projects that, despite short-term losses, by converting to healthy, green food service practices they will soon surpass their old café sales numbers. The NYBG finds that its food and gardening programs are cultivating new audiences and attracting a younger demographic.

Deep engagement is better than a quick hit. If a museum wants to have a long-term impact on any issue, it needs to dig in. This relates to my previous two points as well—the strongest and most productive partnerships develop over time, with the partner organizations making a commitment to long-term cooperation and support. The Children's Museum of Manhattan wants to have a measurable effect on childhood obesity. They started by working with the National Institutes of Health to adapt the NIH *We Can! Obesity* prevention program for an *Early Childhood Obesity Prevention Curriculum.* Now they are partnering with the United Way of New York City and the Administration of Children's Services to integrate these educational methods into Head Start early childhood programs, and with the City University of New York Professional Development Institute to train childcare providers on healthy practices.

Choose your words carefully. Food is generally a safe topic for discussion (as long as you steer clear of impassioned debates about the best ways to make pickles, or BBQ). Obesity, not so much. The Yale Peabody Museum of Natural History considered over 100 potential titles for their exhibit before settling on "Big Food: Health, Culture and the Evolution of Eating" (thus cleverly evoking the issue of size by focusing on portions, not people). Many of the other prospects were, intentionally or not, offensive or off-putting. This sensitivity extended to non-verbal aspects of exhibit design as well—a proposal to contrast a "standard" wheelchair with a bariatric model was nixed when staff realized that this might seem to mock or stigmatize people who need the larger design. The Newark Museum kept its message upbeat by titling its kid-oriented exhibit "Generation Fit: Steps to a Healthier Lifestyle."

Let your audience play a lead role. The Native American community in Arizona suffers from obesity-related diabetes at a rate twice that of the local Anglo-American community. This is due, in large part, to the loss of traditional food and foodways. When staff of the Arizona State Museum decided to help tackle this issue, they had plenty of in-house academic experience to draw upon. But they realized that being right doesn't do any good if you aren't heard, so they challenged Native American and Latino teenagers to develop a comic book (It's Up 2 You!) that takes the message about healthy eating to their peers.

Where Next?

Traditional, object-based museums have long had a conflicted relationship with food. "No food or drink" in the galleries is deeply entrenched in museum culture, sometimes for good reason, sometimes not. Food-related events are often seen as threats to the collections, or as purely income-related opportunities. For the most part, museums are not pre-adapted to use food in their interpretation. The National Museum of the American Indian's Mitsitam Café was designed to showcase Native American foods, but only now, eight years after opening, are staff beginning to bring exhibit elements up to and into the Café's space. Having found, to staff's surprise, that Julia Child's Kitchen was one of its most popular exhibits, the National Museum of American History is now de-installing much of the first floor, including the Kitchen, in order to create a more workable programming space that includes a working demonstration kitchen.

I think the next stage in the co-evolution of museums, food, and community will be the integration of food-related activities into museums' physical space, policies, procedures, and staffing.

Architectural planning for new buildings or renovations will include, from day one, discussions of how and where food might be grown, prepared, and consumed. The food service will be regarded as an element to be designed in concert with the exhibits, echoing and reinforcing their themes. Risk management will give due weight to the benefits of bringing food into the museum, while remaining aware of the potential hazards posed to collections. Museum food service staff will be included in discussions of mission, vision, planning, and interpretation. While the demise of the American Center for Wine Food & the Arts may have marked the last "curator of wine" and "curator of food" for some time to come, we will see more staff positions requiring knowledge of gardening, food history and traditions, food preparation, and community food issues. And with this integration of food into the totality of what they are, museums will find more people joining them at the table.

References

Finkelstein, E.A., Trogdon, J.G., Cohen, J.W., & Dietz, W. (2009). Annual medical spending attributable to obesity: Payer- and service-specific estimates. *Health Affairs* 28(5), w822–w831.

Kosinksi, D. (August 2011). Future of Museums Blog: futureofmuseums.blogspot.com/2011/08/at-phillips-just-take-stairs.html

United Health Foundation, the American Public Health Association and Partnership for Prevention. (2009). The Future costs of obesity: National and state estimates of the impact of obesity on direct health care expenses.

The Good Food Story

From Slavery to the Good Food Revolution

Erika Allen

Abstract
Food is a thread and conduit for culture throughout history. Using a historic perspective, we can examine how the middle passage slave trade, colonialism, the industrial revolution, and the resulting shift from rural to urban migrations have led to our current food system and current economy. Food is more than what we get at the grocery store; it has become an impetus for examining culture, class, and democracy. Museums have the opportunity to weave this story using multidisciplinary, interactive learning spaces where people explore food history timelines.

About the author
Erika Allen is Chicago and National Projects Director for Growing Power and is headquartered in Chicago. She spent her formative years involved in all aspects of farm management, from transplanting seedlings to managing farm stands and farmers' markets. She has been widely recognized for her work with art education and social service, including the Chicago Tribune's Good Eating Award and the Mother of the Environment Award for Minneapolis/St. Paul: she serves on Chicago Mayor Rahm Emmanuel's transition team—Energy, Environment and Public Space Committee. She was most recently appointed as a Commissioner for the Park District. She is the proud mother of 4-year-old son Ayokunle, a Yoruba name meaning "joy fills the home and world."

Museums & Social Issues, Volume 7, Number 1, Spring 2012, pp. 23–27.

Introduction

When we think about food, we often don't think about all of the politics and people who are connected to bringing that food to our tables. We look for the best prices and we look for ingredients to whatever recipe we want to make (whether it's for our dining room table or our kids' lunches). We don't think about all of the politics that go into the choices that we make, or, more importantly and of particular importance to this author, the options that some communities don't have and how the lack of choice is a direct result or symptom of structural racism.

Defining Community Food System

Community food systems are owned by, operated by, and reflect the cultures and cuisines of the people that live within that community food system.

When we talk about good food, we should think not only about the practices the farmer or rancher uses in raising those vegetables or livestock. We also need to include how the workers are treated. Are the workers paid a fair wage? Is the food certified organic? And more importantly, is there ethical treatment of the workers? For example, the Coalition of Immokalee Workers (ciw-online.org/) pressures businesses, from Taco Bell to Trader Joe's and Chipotle, to pay a fair wage to workers, who may not have been visible prior to organizing or becoming activated around something as basic as food. When a community begins thinking about these things, it begins to construct and weave together different parts of the system in ways that food can become a central and pivotal organizing tool.

A community food system includes the entire length of the food chain, from producer to consumer, including transportation and policy regulations, within a community. It encompasses every step of the growing, marketing, and distributing process and evaluates inputs required and outputs produced during all stages of the system. It ensures that the community's needs are met in a sustainable and acceptable fashion. The contemporary, large-scale, industrialized food system largely disregards this aspect of community and functions as a global enterprise requiring the unnecessary expenditure of many finite resources.

Community food systems are a way to organize people to have greater power and democracy within society but also to enhance and enrich quality of life. If a community is able to grow its own food, harvest it, and process it to whatever degree it deems necessary, then it has a lot of power. This is true regardless of a community's economic power. In other words, lots of rich folks do not have food sovereignty. They are dependent on external resources to bring in their food. This includes nations like Canada that import 70% of their food.

This is a revolution in beginning to take back something that's an invisible weapon that people had almost forgotten, a weapon that has become a very valuable commodity, as well as essential to good health and to combating a lot of environmental toxins and challenges within our communities. Community food system work and thought focuses on returning food as a tool for nourishment, medicine, and economic drive that works in balance with ecology and the environment.

The Politics of Food

Occupy the Food System

When I think about a food desert, it's not necessarily just its proximity to the closest big box supermarket; it also includes crime statistics, scores on standardized education tests, unemployment rates, foreclosure rates, and all of the benchmarks of a community that has been disenfranchised. If we include those benchmarks in the dynamics around what a food desert is, and we talk about "occupying the food system"— using food as an organizing tool for people to address these larger dynamics—then the food movement is a very powerful revolution.

The food movement is a great opportunity for museums and other entities that tell stories to frame the visitors' experience using objects and information around food. Museums can present food as a powerful political indicator and cultural barometer, with many narratives and points of view.

The *Occupy* movement, which started in New York to protest social and economic inequities, has since spread around the world, applying pressure in a number of fields, including economics, education, peacekeeping, and, of course, food—including a few marches by farmers and food activists to use protest as a way to change the way that people eat.

Food, Culture, and Spirit

Food can also have a spiritual element. Many cultures offer food to their ancestors, and many indigenous cultures literally feed the divinities. Food and spirituality are connected with food sovereignty and political movements through efforts such as the *Growing Food and Justice for All Initiative* (www.growingfoodandjustice.org/) that has a working group called Food, Culture, and Spirit. The reclamation of one's food sovereignty and food practices restores culture and can create new cultural dynamics that bring together people from different walks of life and ethnic backgrounds to form new alliances. Food and spirituality can also be pivotal in restorative experiences becoming a part of professional development seminars, intense anti-racism training, and analysis of food desert communities. Museums have an opportunity to tell these stories in powerful ways, linking the land with both the consumption of food by humans and ritualistically by the divinities.

History of Food

A Story of Oppression, Cultural Preservation, and Revolution

I have long been interested in the unspoken legacy of how our food system is very much based on the slave trade and the economies of both the South and the North. We couldn't have the kind of agriculture or built the wealth and global economy for the past 400 years without slavery. The parallel story is a story of cultural preservation. People who were slaves were able to replicate traditional dishes with different ingredients here in the Americas and Caribbean. Slaves were sometimes able to smuggle seeds, and some of the plants were cultivated here. Making chitlins, or pigs feet, or eating ribs or foods that are not created with the higher quality cuts of meat pays homage to our ancestors who were able to survive eating those foods. These foods are now ingrained in our culture, helping us find who we are. Now we're moving into a time where we're able to travel back to the Motherland to experience what those foods are like in their traditional preparations, which are often healthy, non-meat based, and connected to cultural ritual and natural cycles. It's amazing how we can trace the thread of foods across the ocean.

Conclusion

Finally, the revolutionary component. The Good Food Revolution is a reflection of a pivotal time in history where people are reclaiming their food and agricultural heritage and using it as a tool for social change. We have the opportunity to live in communities that are nurturing and respectful of the earth. A community that is able to work in balance with nature tends to not be as violent and tends to not have as many of the symptoms of violence or the layers of oppression or racism. That's the revolution.

Cooking Our Native Landscapes, Eating Our Indigenous Cultures

Enrique Salmon

Abstract

Indigenous people around the world still subsist on much of what they can grow. Their practices and agricultural traditions maintain crucial legacies on the landscapes that they manage. Thousands of varieties of unique vegetables, fruits, and livestock depend on the indigenous farmers that continue to husband them. Many of these crops, such as corn, would revert to their pre-human state within a few years if not for human manipulations that maintain their present forms. These varieties of plants and animals retain our human legacy and our contribution to diversity so long as we maintain our relationship to the landscapes where we live.

About the author

Enrique Salmón is Head of the American Indian Studies Program at Cal State University, East Bay, located in Hayward, California. He has a PhD in Anthropology from Arizona State University. Enrique has published several articles and chapters on indigenous ethnobotany, agriculture, nutrition, and traditional ecological knowledge, including his book *Eating the Landscape: American Indian Stewards of Food and Resilience*, the source of many of the ideas included here.

Museums & Social Issues, Volume 7, Number 1, Spring 2012, pp. 29–39.

I was born into and raised by a big Mexican-Indian family. We continue a tradition dating back centuries—we grow much of our own food. Grandma always maintained her collection of special herbs while, my grandfather grew his small fruit orchard, corn, and *nopalitos* (prickly pear cactus) that were all important ingredients in many meals. Food was an essential ingredient at all family gatherings. It blended with music, teasing, laughter, stories, and dancing to create a delicious pungent celebration. Our celebrations were sometimes planned, but more often than not, impromptu gatherings spurred by a cousin getting a new job, Dad getting a raise, or a family member having just returned from being gone for a length of time. Once it was decided that a celebration was in order someone would soon ask, "What are we going to eat?"

Sometimes the food itself would be cause for celebration. Every now and then Aunt Nick would bring over a bag of freshly picked avocados. To this day I don't know where they came from or how she came to get the avocados, but she would just show up with a plain paper bag of about 20 avocados ready to be transformed into guacamole or simply sliced and to eaten with salt, pepper, and salsa. She never knocked on the door or announced herself when she came into our little home. She would just enter, set the bag of avocados on the nearest flat surface and gruffly greet my mom or me. It was assumed by all that the fruits would be made into something to eat on the spot. Magically a feast was set before us and we were eating and laughing. There was always something to eat at our home even if it was just tortillas and beans; it was a requirement.

Our family gatherings were and are loving and soulful times. Food, especially foods made by the hands of the people present, added to the soulful and loving feelings inherent in the space. Every day our food included tortillas, beans, and some kind of burritos or tacos. We did not know that fajitas would someday become haute cuisine. My mom's tortillas were always near perfect circles. They were soft and pliable and smelled best when I was returning home from a long day of being outside with my cousins. I could smell the aroma while still outside letting my bicycle crash to the ground. Entering the house I would inhale deeply in order to gloriously embrace the warmth of corn and flour masa being heated, pinto beans steaming on the stove, and a flimsy pile of newly cooked tortillas on the table behind where my mom stood by the oven. I enjoyed the fresh tortillas most with melted butter rolled up inside the hot circle. They also tasted great with a simple bowl of pinto beans swimming in the juices ladled into the bowl from the pot.

Cooking pinto beans were both a simple and complex affair. I never ate canned beans until I left home, and when I finally did, they were unsatisfactory. Pinto beans prepared from scratch required only the hard, uncooked beans. They were spread on a table and sifted for stones, dirt clods, and those wrinkled up beans that appeared as if they had shriveled up in the sun. Then they were prepared with pig's feet or salt pork, lard, epazote, and other secret spices. A pot of beans was more like a stew than a staple dish.

Foods that require an extra process before preparation, such as beans, corn, and whole grains, provide both a brush of texture and color to meal preparation and further community involvement in their process from harvest to meal. When helping my mom sort the hidden stones from the beans I used to place a single shiny bean inside my mouth and flick it with my tongue in order to bounce it against the insides of my teeth. I sometimes wondered if I did that long enough or if I accidentally swallowed the bean if a plant would begin to sprout inside my body. My mom used to warn me that the beans were dirty and worried that I would get sick. I figured that I had swallowed so many germs already in my daily activities as a kid that one semi-dirty bean wouldn't cause any more harm. I knew where the beans had come from. In some cases I helped collect beans from their semi-dried and dried encasements hanging from their stalks. This kind of tactile knowledge contributed to my overall library of food-related knowledge. Strangely, I would not be able to identify the source of most of my food knowledge from my childhood. I just simply knew it. It has become part of the volumes of the library of traditional knowledge encoded in the language of my family experiences and added to during later interactions with land-based indigenous people.

Of course, we ate our family version of tacos, tostadas, burritos, and other northern Mexican cuisine, but it would be difficult to compare our version of these dishes to those in a typical Mexican restaurant. This is because the preparation and ingredients associated with these foods reflected our unique collective family history and experiences, especially those connected to landscapes.

When the occasion was more than impromptu, the King and Queen of celebration foods emerged; carne asada and tamales. Carne asada—beef strips marinated in various blends of spices, citrus juices, and herbs—would cause my first cousin's mouth to water at its very mention. Beer was an essential accompaniment with carne asada. We would drive miles out of our way to find the very best carne asada either pre-prepared and brought home in plastic bags while still marinating, or cooked and speedily couriered by a relative to the party location. It was best cooked outside over a barbeque and eaten with tortillas. Tamales arrived on a plate in front of the eater in a variety of incarnations depending on which member of the family had supervised the preparation. One could identify the maker by his or her signature ingredients, softness of the corn masa, and amount of filling. One never dared mention a preference of tamales in public for fear of some kind of familial retribution. Besides, they were all good, and recipes were often amalgams of several current and past family members' recipes. Still, there was this underlying competition surrounding tamales that was pursued by the tamale chefs in the family. In our case, it included most of the married women. Although they all preached the beauty and love associated with the fact that the important thing was that we all had enough to eat, I recall watching my various aunts eyeing us as we ate their tamales. They paid attention to the ephemeral qualities of the gusto we poured into our tamale eating. They secretly counted how many of their or their sisters' tamales we ate, and if we made comments or other such eating related noises. I never told anyone, especially my mom, but I really enjoyed most the tamales made by her best friend, Eloisa. She was not a blood relative, and became a friend of my mom when I was very young after we moved into Eloisa's

Woman at a local food market, Oaxaca, Mexico.
Photo courtesy of author.

neighborhood. Eloisa's tamales were always moist and could be counted on to contain a hefty spicy pork filling offset by the unusual inclusion of raisins. The raisins were unique and special. I can still recall the first time I bit into her tamales. At first my mouth was surprised at the squirt of raisin juice amongst the familiar spices and textures. Quickly, I realized the ingredient and have searched for this kind of tamales ever since.

Recipes were shared during celebrations and whenever family came together. They are a form of knowledge reproduction and social exchange. They gave everyone something to talk and gossip about, to share, and to be proud of. Without the sharing of recipes the family community begins to dissolve. The tamale making parties are less frequent. No one has time to spend preparing the masa and to get together. Anniversaries and weddings have to be planned a year in advance. Today in many neighborhoods where there is a large Hispanic community nearby couples walk the street holding between them a large pressure cooker or ice chest filled with hot tamales. They arrive at the front doors of stranger's homes selling the contents of their burden in order to make ends meet. What was once a celebration food has become a source of supplementary income.

I have eaten my share of tamales, but more often than not I have no idea who made them and under what circumstances. Perhaps laughter accompanied the making; I would hope. Nevertheless, these tamales do not connect me to a community. My identity and culture as a Mexican-Indian is reaffirmed whenever I eat tamales, but not the unique community with whom I grew up and from where my understanding of my identity and its connection to a landscape emerged. My reaffirmation of identity and connection to place is not a direct result of the tamales, but comes more from the processes that surround tamales, beans, raisins inside of tamales, and my grandmother's herbal teas. The processes interconnect family, landscape, collection knowledge, story, and an encoded library of cultural and ecological knowledge, all of which sustain and revitalize a sense of self and place. A statistic I read on a back of a milk carton one morning revealed that people who ate so many meals with their families suffered less from crimes and other social ills. This milk-carton morality reflects, I feel, the consequences of modern society that is removed from a direct relationship to its food and from the social process related to "eating a landscape."

Eating a landscape is more than the act of eating. Eating a landscape is also a socially reaffirming act. In the case of my family whenever I eat Eloisa's tamales recipe or my mother's salsa, I am eating the memories and knowledge associated with those foods. The elements of the stories, the jokes, and the intricate contextualized experience become embodied every time the eating takes place. It becomes a form of mimetic regeneration to eat meals prepared from family recipes.

Eating is also a cultural act that reaffirms one's identity and worldview each time we sit down to a plate of home cooked beans, or *sopa de albondigas*. Culture is performed by humans every minute of every day. Eating our culture and our familial memories is another ritual that is acted throughout our lives. How we remember our lines for this ongoing stage act happens each time we prepare to do something cultural, like eating old family recipes. In other words, we often eat our culture and our land. Leslie Marmon Silko (1996) reminds us in *Yellow Woman and Beauty of the Spirit* that we "depend upon the collective memory through successive generations to maintain and transmit an entire culture, a worldview complete with proven strategies for survival." We have to eat in order to survive; therefore, food becomes a medium through which a complex of collective memory from generations of preparing tamales remains alive and intact.

Food landscapes remain intact when old recipes are regenerated. The food itself, and the landscapes from which it emerges, remembers how it should be cooked. This can happen because the food itself activates in us an encoded memory that reminds us how to grow, collect, and prepare the food. The land and food then become the source of knowledge and history. Many recipes are dynamic. They get altered and tailored to family changes, history, and events. Often a family member will alter the recipe, or someone new to the family will cause this to happen. The specific family members might change, but the food and the land where it is grows remain the source of the cultural memory. Each recipe addition is valuable as it adds to the continuous composition of the culture and family. The recipes act like stories that are told and retold in different ways depending on the storyteller, or in this case, the cook. Because they are family recipes they are also communal. Communal storytelling has a way of correcting itself. The corrections are not seeking absolute truth, but communal truth. As example is when Aunt Nick might remind Aunt Vera that that wasn't the spice that Grandma used in the salsa, and then Vera responds with a correction from a different experience and point in family history. These kinds of debates are not merely family disputes or arguments, but act as self-correcting landmarks and also as mediums through which critical family history is recounted and corrected.

I do most of the cooking in my home. I prepare dishes cooked by my family for decades. It is a way of continuing the story of the family and cultural way of interacting with a landscape and with eating. A recipe can embody everything that is important to a family and even a culture. Just recently a friend and her husband came over for dinner. My wife and I prepared, among many things, some guacamole. Our friend was overwhelmed by how good the guacamole was and asked for the recipe. I realized that I really never follow a recipe when I prepare dishes such as guacamole. I retell myself stories from family events of the past. In those stories I single out how particular family members prepared their versions of the dish. In this process I am performing a cultural and familial remembering. Recently, however, I have realized that those old family dishes are part of a much larger cuisine unique to North America. It is a complex and sophisticated cuisine that matches cuisines from around the world.

A New American Indian Cuisine

Today there is a growing group of American Indian and nonnative activists who are devoted to identifying producers across the country that are hanging onto or reviving foods and foodways that have been present in North America since before the arrival of Europeans. These food traditions rely on a myriad of ingredients native to North American landscapes and often involve complex preparation. I have always mentioned to anyone within earshot that foods such as mole-negro are nearest to the type of intricate foods that meso-americans consumed when Europeans first floundered their way into North America. Mole is a complex dish fully representative of the landscape and agricultural system cultivated by Central Americans. The list of ingredients and the numerous steps involved in producing even a simple mole is multifaceted enough to cause any culinary student pause.

American Indian foods require unique preparatory steps, agricultural techniques, harvesting rules, and even eating rituals such as many devoted to corn. In essence this is cuisine. At one level posole is simply a stew of corn, spices, and sometimes bits of meat, depending on the region and even the family that is preparing the dish. Approached with preparation in mind, posole requires a specified manner of first growing a certain type of corn hybridized over centuries to fit the tastes that Native people have come to appreciate in a bowl of posole. As a result, posole is also the kind of corn that is used in the preparation of the dish. The term activates a mental blend in the minds of people culturally familiar with this kind of food.

Posole preparation employs dried hominy corn that has had its hulls removed. The corn is soaked in water overnight. The next day the corn is placed in a cooking pot that cannot be metal or at least it must be an enameled pot. This requirement is essential to the process because the next step involves the addition of culinary ash that reacts negatively to metal. Culinary ash is the white ash left over from the complete burning of certain types of woods. Depending on the culture and on what foods are being prepared the ash may be from saltbush, juniper, or even bean plants. The lye and alkali present in the ash have a way of making the niacin present in the corn available for the human digestive process and also change the color and consistency of the corn. After boiling for about five hours the hominy is cooled under running water while one's fingers work to remove the hulls. Next, the hominy is dried again and stored for later use. One can appreciate from this description that Native foods are beyond simple ones that are only raised, harvested, dried, and then eaten. The foods involve a process that reflects centuries of creativity and innovation.

Another innovative and equally complex Southwestern food is piki bread. Prior to European contact Native North Americans did not know sourdough, ciabatta, or even seven-grain flax/oatmeal breads. The nearest things to bread-like foods were corn tortillas, tamales, and what the Hopi came to know as piki. Piki comes in newsprint-thin sheets of cooked batter rolled up and served at special occasions. Making piki requires both art and skill. Young Hopi brides must demonstrate their adeptness at making piki prior to being considered suitable to be married. Piki is "baked" in special piki houses on flat stones that have been seasoned. Piki stones become family treasures handed down through several generations. The thick stone rests elevated above smaller stones, normally at the edge or corner of a piki house. Cedar branches are burnt under the stone during the cooking process. The batter consists of water, normally blue cornmeal, and culinary ash. Sometimes yellow and white cornmeal is used depending on the ceremonial purpose. The thin batter, the consistency of runny pancake batter, is spread on the stone with the bare hands of the adept chef. It takes years to master the technique while losing a few layers of fingertip skin. The batter is rubbed onto the stone in layers. When dried to the proper consistency, the layers are peeled off the stone into one sheet and then rolled up. After the cooking process, and while the stone remains hot, the stone is "greased" with ground up watermelon or squash seeds. The natural oils from the seeds seep into the stone. Eating piki is an art in itself. One bite into the bread results in a shower of crumbs down the front of the eater. I often surrender to my messiness as a piki eater or attempt to take small bites that don't seem to result is fewer crumbs. I have also tried the dip and bite approach where one dips the end of the bread into a stew or sauce and then bites into it. The result is often the same, but it sure is fun.

When piki is served or is present on a table, the result is often many smiles and elevated conversation, especially from Hopi and other Pueblo peoples. Piki is one of those special occasion foods that transports people to moments in time captured in the memory and uploaded by certain smells and sites. These stored moments are normally pleasant ones, often from childhood. Piki acts as mental refugia of cultural memory, cultural survival, and identity. Piki can even activate ecological knowledge related to agricultural techniques and wild crafting culinary ash. Piki can blend with other refugia foods, creating mosaics of cultural memory.

Another such food that evokes a concert of cultural and sensual reaction from peoples from the Southwest and also one of the simplest is roasted green chili. Mention roasted green chili to any native of the American Southwest, whether Hispano, Indigenous, or Anglo, and then plan for reactions ranging from sheer ambrosia to distain and a litany of stories and anecdotes from the funny and absurd to soulful and spiritual.

A variety of chili that exists in the northwest Mexico where my people are from is the chiltepin. It is also known as chili pequin. This is a tiny red pepper that in maturity grows erect on small bushes in the wild. The fruits are about the size of a one's pinky fingernail. My grandmother used to grow these tiny balls of fire in our field. She would grind about two of them up to add to a pot of beans or a stew. That was enough to change a bland pot of beans into a mouth-stimulating dish.

Chiltepins are highly respected in Northwest Mexico to the point where unique chiltepin grinding contraptions can be found on family dinning tables. They are carved from ironwood in creative shapes and designs. The working part is a simple hole drilled into the top of the tool with a long plug resting in the hole. The plug has some teeth carved into its working end. As with other chilis one has to be careful when handling chitepins. An errant touch to one's lips, eyes, or nose can result in irritation for an hour or so due to the irritant, capsiasin, found to varying degrees in all chilis. People in places like Sonora, Mexico, however, like to crunch the small dried peppers into their meals. One way they have dealt with avoiding the irritation is to use a grinding contraption. The chiltepin is placed into the hole, the plug is placed in the hole on top of the pepper and then twisted around for a couple of seconds. The plug is removed and the ground pepper can now be safely poured into one's foods.

Foods like chili, piki bread, and posole are contemporary markers of our human legacy. They are final products of processes that dynamically reflect the human/land relationships across the continent, and they reflect our continued efforts to blend past and present while we reach for a future where our cultural flavors and colors enhance the beauty of the landscapes with which we live and whose stewardship has been bestowed upon us.

Reference

Silko, L. M. (1996). *Yellow woman and a beauty of the spirit.* New York: Simon and Shuster.

What's Cooking, Uncle Sam?

Alice Kamps, Tom Nastick, Susan Clifton, Rebecca Martin

Abstract

In June 2011 the National Archives unveiled *What's Cooking, Uncle Sam?,* an exhibition of records tracing the government's effect on the American diet. It was the first National Archives exhibition to explore the topic of food and , as we discovered, it was a topic that opened many doors. Due to his personal interest in the subject, we formed a unique partnership with a local celebrity chef, José Andrés. Chef Andrés opened a companion restaurant to the exhibition and participated in the National Archives' *America Eats* program series. The richness of the content and the currency of the issues, together with Chef Andrés's involvement, resulted in unprecedented interest from the media and the public, raising the profile of the National Archives locally, nationally, and internationally. As a result, the exhibition, programming series, and social media initiatives were able to tap into a variety of new audiences for the National Archives.

About the authors

The four authors work at the National Archives in Washington, DC. Alice Kamps, Curator, researched and developed the show and wrote the script and accompanying publications. Tom Nastick, Public Program Producer/Theater Manager, and Susan Clifton, Public Programs Producer, created and implemented the program series. Rebecca Martin, Coordinator, oversaw the creation and maintenance of the Wiki, Tumblr account, and other social media applications.

Museums & Social Issues, Volume 7, Number 1, Spring 2012, pp. 41–49.

The Exhibition

What's Cooking, Uncle Sam? was on exhibit in the Lawrence F. O'Brien Gallery at the National Archives in Washington, DC, from June 10, 2011, to January 3, 2012. After decades of discovering fascinating records about food, Christina Rudy Smith, the Director of Exhibitions, chose to mount a temporary exhibition on the topic of food. Given the pervasiveness of media coverage on food safety, regulation, nutrition, cooking, and agriculture over the past several years, the exhibition had the potential to appeal to a wide audience. In addition, one of the goals of the National Archives' temporary exhibition program is to open visitors' eyes to the breadth and scope of the records it holds in trust for the American people. The fact that food is a topic of many government records was unexpected for some who associate the National Archives with the Declaration of Independence and the rarefied atmosphere of the Rotunda. The exhibition department hoped that *What's Cooking, Uncle Sam?* would communicate the message that government records touch on almost every aspect of our lives.

Entrance to *What's Cooking, Uncle Sam?* *Photo courtesy of the National Archives.*

Spanning the Revolutionary War era through the late 1900s, the records in the exhibition echoed many of our current concerns about government's role in the health and safety of our food supply. Described as a "must-see show" on the website Smithsonian.com, *What's Cooking, Uncle Sam?* featured over 100 original records—including folk songs, a model train car, war posters, educational films, 19th century food labels, nutrition guides, Congressional acts, and seed packets. The records were grouped in four areas. 1) *Farm* explored the ways that government has affected what farmers grow, farming methods, and agricultural markets. This area featured documentation of the expeditions undertaken by plant explorer Frank N. Meyer, records from the seed distribution program, and experiment stations. 2) *Factory* traced the origins of the Pure Food and Drug Act and the Meat Inspection Act, including an original letter from Upton Sinclair to President Theodore Roosevelt and records from "the Poison Squad," Harvey Wiley's experiment about the effects of food adulterants on human volunteers. 3) *Kitchen* opened with the early nutrition research performed by Wilbur Atwater and the subsequent nutrition guides published by the government. Also on display in this area were posters and artifacts from wartime food campaigns, including a memo written by Margaret Mead during her tenure as Secretary of the Committee on Food Habits. 4) *Table* covered military food and the school lunch program, as well as Americans' fascination with what our presidents eat. Of interest in this area was the Revolutionary War era rations broadside and a letter from Queen Elizabeth II to President Eisenhower enclosing her recipe for scones.

The Chef

Named "Outstanding Chef" by the James Beard Foundation in 2011, José Andrés is an internationally-recognized chef/owner of ThinkFoodGroup and advocate for food and hunger issues. Andrés grew up outside of Barcelona and made his way to the United States as a young man. He eagerly adopted his new country and became fascinated with the culinary history of the United States. He was excited to collaborate with us on *What's*

Cooking, Uncle Sam? and offered to open a companion restaurant to the exhibit exploring the culinary history of the United States. *America Eats* Tavern opened on July 4, 2011 on 8th Street NW, across the street from the National Archives. Named after the Works Progress Administration (WPA) writers project of the 1930s, *America Eats* offered a new take on American classics and celebrated native ingredients and some long forgotten dishes, from burgoo to oysters Rockefeller. The restaurant provided the unique opportunity for visitors to enhance their experience of the exhibition through their taste buds. The restaurant was ultimately a benefit, with proceeds from the restaurant donated to the Foundation to support the educational efforts of the National Archives. As part of the collaboration, Andrés also contributed to both the exhibit catalog and recipe book, *Eating with Uncle Sam,* and participated in a series of public programs, the "America Eats" series that offered discussions on the role of government in our daily diet.

Media Coverage

The media's interest in *What's Cooking, Uncle Sam?* was immediate, intense, and prolonged. It was immediately apparent that we had struck upon a topic of interest to a wide variety of types of media, from newspapers (*New York Times, Wall Street Journal, USA Today,* and *Washington Post*) to radio and television (NPR's *Morning Edition,* ABC's *World News Tonite,* and *CNN*) to the blogosphere (*Huffington Post, Salon.com, the Atlantic*). The media coverage was much more extensive than other temporary exhibitions at the National Archives had received.

Public Programs

The Washington, DC-area Public Programs Team within NARA's Legislative Archives, Presidential Libraries and Museum Services Division produced an unprecedented 36 programs related to *What's Cooking, Uncle Sam?*—the most ever connected to a single exhibit. An eclectic mix of panel discussions, film programs, book lectures, performances —even a game show—was presented to

Three former White House chefs discuss their experiences cooking for the presidents and their families. (*Seated left to right*) Roland Mesnier, Frank Ruta, Pierre Chambrin, and NPR's Susan Stamberg (moderator). *Photo courtesy of the National Archives.*

over 4,400 patrons in the elegant William G. McGowan Theater. In the spirit of the exhibition, the wide range of topics explored included food safety, agriculture policy, feeding the military, ethnic cooking, historical figures such as John Chapman (better known as Johnny Appleseed) and Fred Harvey, even where to find the best burgers in America.

Highlights included the "America Eats" series of panel discussions featuring celebrity Chef Jose Andrés; screening and discussions of important documentary films including Pare Lorentz' 1936 classic *The Plow That Broke the Plains,* the 2008 Oscar-nominated documentary *Food, Inc.* (presented as part of the ongoing partnership with the Academy of Motion Picture Arts & Sciences), and 2010's *Lunch Line*; a series of Saturday matinee screenings of Hollywood feature films with food themes; an open house on the museum level presented in participation with Food Day, a nationwide initiative of the Center for Science in the Public Interest that featured representatives from the USDA, the FDA, Mars, Inc., and other organizations; a presentation of *Archives Jeopardy!* hosted by Archivist of the United States David

S. Ferriero; and a rare on-stage gathering for former White House Chefs Roland Mesnier, Pierre Chambrin, and Frank Ruta.

Taking full advantage of the innovative food and culinary related programming schedule, the public programs team reached out to new audiences by marketing to culinary schools, food writers, gourmet tourism, culinary magazines and publications, nutrition schools and centers, and local restaurants. A variety of marketing vehicles and methods were utilized, including targeted mailings of specially designed postcards, social media efforts for FaceBook, Twitter, YouTube and blogs; the National Archives website; the National Archives printed calendar of events, mailed to 8,000 households in the Washington, DC, metro area; targeted email blasts to over 5,000 recipients; and paid newspaper advertising. Prior to some of the public programs, speakers wrote guest posts for the National Archives blog, generating interest and creating buzz.

Exciting new partnerships were cultivated to enhance and cross-promote the programming, creating more opportunities to reach new audiences. The Mexican Embassy and Cultural Institute enthusiastically supported the program featuring Mexican cooking legend, Diana Kennedy. The partnership with Jose Andrés's Think Food Group resulted in six programs mostly focusing on important food and agricultural issues. In partnership with Applegate Farms, the national school lunch program was discussed. A number of programs were produced in partnership with the United States Department of Agriculture and the Food and Drug Administration. Food for the military was addressed in partnership with the U.S. Army Research, Development and Engineering Center. Jewish cooking was featured in partnership with the Jewish Historical Society of Greater Washington, and 18th century food and chocolate were presented in partnership with Mount Vernon and the Mars Historic Chocolate Division.

Social Media Initiatives

Staff at the National Archives planned social media initiatives with several goals in mind:

- To alert regular supporters of the National Archives about the exhibition and then, throughout "What's Cooking's" run, to keep it on potential visitors' minds
- To make exhibition material available to people who were unable to visit "What's Cooking"
- To showcase items from the Archives holdings that did not make it into the exhibition
- To build new—real and virtual—audiences for the National Archives

Communications, exhibits, education, and social media staff members all worked together to post material on agency blogs, Facebook pages, Twitter feeds, Flickr streams, and Tumblrs. Food was a perfect topic for social media activities, perhaps because eating, cooking, and shopping for food are such social activities for many people. Many of the food-related posts captured the attention and imagination of people all across the country, generating responses in all of these spaces.

One of the first posts related to "What's Cooking" promoted the exhibition several weeks before it opened. In honor of the wedding of Prince William and Kate Middleton, the Archives issued a press release that asked "Fretting over your royal wedding breakfast?" and invited readers to examine one of the documents featured in the exhibition, a scone recipe sent by Queen Elizabeth to Dwight Eisenhower after the president's 1959 visit to Balmoral Castle. The press release was distributed to the media and made available on www.archives.gov on April 25, 2011. Two days later, an Archives blog post included the document showing the recipe, the story of the president's visit, and a photo of the president and Queen Elizabeth. The Archives tweeted about the blog entry and linked to it from the public affairs office's Facebook page. One of the regional facilities of the Archives posted the item on its Facebook page that same day. The document was also published on Scribd. A few weeks later, when members of the press were invited to preview the exhibition, staff posted on Flickr an image of the favors distributed at the event: gift bags of individual scones and the recipe. The Flickr post linked to the copy of the document in Scribd.

All of this blogging, tweeting, Facebook posting, and so forth—combined with the press release—caused a flurry of activity on the web. Food bloggers posted the document and their own translations of the recipe, as well as their reports about their successes and failures in making the scones. A television station in New Haven, Connecticut, produced a segment on the recipe and then posted the story on its website, and the recipe ended up on Good Morning America's website. Most of the time, when someone wrote about the document, the writer linked to one of the pages on the National Archives website showing the document. And in most instances, 5 to 60 other people forwarded the post, commented on it, liked it, or tweeted about it. Over the next six months, this single document generated dozens of discussions on topics such as what is a "drop scone," the American translation of English recipe ingredients, and how to cook the scones (in the oven or on a griddle). People re-wrote the recipe; they offered their own favorite scone recipes; they published photographs of the scones they had made using the original or altered recipe; they suggested toppings; and they suggested appropriate beverages.

The Archives posted the most material related to "What's Cooking, Uncle Sam?" on one of its Tumblr sites: www.usnatarchivesexhibits.tumblr.com. Each of the 279 posts on the site, from the opening of the exhibition to its close on January 3, 2012, was connected to food. Most of these posts featured items that were not on view in the exhibition, so publishing them on the Tumblr site was the primary way to publicize these documents and photographs.

Measuring the reach of material that is published on social media sites is difficult, as we cannot know, for instance, how many people view a particular post and how many people follow each person who re-blogs an item. Posts that appealed to readers' quirky senses of humor often garnered the most attention. A photo of a cat lapping at a man's beer as he slumps into sleep in a bar received 91 "notes." Examining these notes can give a sense that the posts have a far wider reach than is apparent from the number of followers. Of the 91 notes, 34 indicated that another Tumblr user reblogged the post. More than half of the rebloggers were reblogging from a third party, rather than from the original post. The notes show that in several cases, the post followed a chain of reblogging, being passed from one person's tumblr onto several subsequent blogs.

The tumblr certainly seemed to develop a following. When it began, the site had zero followers. At the time of the final "What's Cooking" post, the number had increased to 3,261. This increase in attention is made apparent also by the increase in the number of notes. At the end of the exhibition's first month, the tumblr had a total of 158 notes in response to the documents, photographs, audio, and motion picture recordings. In November, the month with the most activity from viewers, 2,464 notes appeared on the site.

While we do not know the identity of the people who follow or simply view the tumblr, we do know basic demographic information about tumblr users. Since tumblrs are more ethnically diverse than survey data indicate National Archives visitors are, and since they skew more to the 18–34 age range than the Archives' visitor pool does, reaching people through Tumblr seems to widen significantly the audience of the institution.

Conclusion

The National Archives exhibition *What's Cooking, Uncle Sam?* was created on a modest budget: approximately $200,000 for 3,000 square feet. But the effect it had our audience and media coverage was enormous. The impact was a factor of the public's interest in the topic: food. By building an exhibition, program series, and social media interactives on a variety of subjects related to food, the National Archives tapped into the energy and creativity of many new community partners, media outlets, and audiences. It stimulated discussion online, in the gallery, at our programming events, and in the media. It demonstrated that if a museum or cultural institution has a contribution to make to a conversation of current interest to the public, food for example, the public will find multiple ways to engage with it.

Cape Cod Children's Museum's Little Sprouts Kids' Garden

Lori Lieberman

Abstract

In 2005, Cape Cod Children's Museum in Mashpee, Massachusetts, developed the Little Sprouts Kids' Garden in partnership with Coonamessett Farm, a farm and research enterprise located in nearby East Falmouth. This case study article describes how the museum and farm partner to create programming that connects children to the agricultural heritage of Cape Cod. *Little Sprouts Kids' Garden* is a hands-on informal learning program that focuses on gardening and farm experiences for children 3 to 10 years of age. Children participate in organic gardening and learn about good nutrition, the value of local sustainable agriculture, and the rhythms of the natural world. A summary of how this program has impacted the local community is included, and tips on how other children's museums might replicate this program are outlined.

About the author

Lori Lieberman is Director of Arts and Agriculture at Cape Cod Children's Museum. Lieberman's case study was first published in 2010 by the Association of Children's Museums (ACM) in the publication *Healthy Kids, Healthy Museums.* This edited version is provided with permission by ACM: www.ChildrensMuseums.org.

Museums & Social Issues, Volume 7, Number 1, Spring 2012, pp. 51–57.

Cape Cod Children's Museum's mission is to provide a learning environment that stimulates curiosity, creativity, and imagination and inspires children and their families to engage with each other, their community, and the world at large. Healthy practices are central to the philosophy of the museum, encouraging families to play and explore together and offering programs and resources to support healthy choices. Opened in 1992 in the town of Mashpee, Massachusetts, Cape Cod Children's Museum is the only children's museum on Cape Cod.

Cape Cod's heritage centered on the fishing and whaling industries, but agriculture also played a major role in its history. Farmers on the Cape raised cattle and sheep and grew produce on its rich farmland to supply urban areas such as Boston. Today, little agricultural land remains on Cape Cod, and there are few working farms. As a result, many children are disconnected from the source of their food, unaware that it is possible and desirable to grow their own food rather than purchasing it from a supermarket. Children do not necessarily have relatives or neighbors able to share their knowledge or expertise as in past generations, when growing a garden and raising farm animals at home was common practice.

Despite these cultural and land-use changes, Cape Cod Children's Museum also detected that the community it serves had a palatable and growing awareness of organic and local food production and a strong interest in the Cape's agricultural heritage. Museum staff mused: What if a flock of free-range chickens encountered on the way to pick cucumbers are the same chickens that children incubated and raised from farm-gathered fresh eggs the previous summer? What if, after a lesson about pollination, children watch the beekeeper as he arrives unannounced to check on his hives, wearing his netted hat and gear? How could the museum incorporate these kinds of natural encounters with its hands-on, interactive museum learning experiences?

The museum found its answer to incorporate authentic nature encounters with its informal learning strategies by partnering with Coonamessett Farm, located in nearby East Falmouth. Founded in 1989, the farm is comprised of 20 acres of fields and greenhouses offering a variety of vegetables, herbs, berries and flowers. Farm animals include goats, sheep, donkeys, alpacas, chickens, ducks and rabbits.

Together in the summer of 2005, the two organizations introduced *Little Sprouts*. This hands-on program, held on the farm premises, focuses on gardening and farm activities with a major emphasis on the garden that the children design, plant, maintain, and harvest. Children learn about organic gardening methods, good nutrition, the value of local sustainable agriculture, and the beauty of connecting to the seasons and the rhythms of the natural world. Classes include farm- and garden-related arts and crafts, science projects, stories, games, and special activities. Participating children grow and harvest a wide assortment of organic vegetables, berries, fruits, and herbs that they share with their families throughout the growing season. During class, children spend the majority of the time outdoors regardless of the weather, working in the garden or engaged in activities elsewhere on the farm. Class time includes nature walks on the premises, visits with the farm animals, and excursions to the farm fields for picking and learning about the wide variety of available fresh produce. Rather than watching the natural world on a television or computer screen, *Little Sprouts* participants are directly immersed in it, whether planting seeds, observing a bee hive, discovering insects in the garden, feeding the chickens, or measuring rainfall.

Measuring Impact

Little Sprouts' success has been measured through written evaluations (requested from participating families at the end of each session), repeat attendance, the addition of younger siblings, and fully enrolled sessions with a waiting list. Many participating families have reported positive lifestyle changes in terms of nutrition and meal planning, and several have built gardens at home, putting into practice all that the children have learned at *Little Sprouts*. Almost all of the enrolled families have become members of Coonamessett Farm and regularly visit to enjoy outdoor family time together while exploring the premises, visiting the farm animals, harvesting fresh farm produce, or gathering eggs from the chickens and ducks.

Because the children are immersed in farm life during their participation in *Little Sprouts,* they acquire a unique appreciation for all aspects of the farm's seasonal cycle. The farm and garden work done during classes—in sunshine and in rain—parallels the ongoing efforts of the farm workers. The *Little Sprouts* garden reflects the seasonal development of the surrounding farm fields from start to finish, from empty garden rows in the spring right through to sowing a cover crop of rye grass to prepare for the winter. The children observe natural processes such as the birth and growth of farm animals, the sprouting-fruiting-cyclical completion of plants, and unanticipated but natural problems such as insect damage and plant disease—all part of agricultural life past and present.

Building community is an essential aspect of *Little Sprouts.* Children do not have their own individual garden plots to care for but instead work together to create a beautiful and productive experience to share with each other and their families. Community spirit is also an important part of the program's end of summer harvest celebration, when the children gather produce from the *Little Sprouts* garden, not for themselves but for the local food pantry.

Describing the Program

The *Little Sprouts* partnership is a shared enterprise. The Cape Cod Children's Museum is responsible for providing staff, marketing and publicity, art and science supplies, and bookkeeping/accounting. Coonamessett Farm provides garden space, water, plants and seeds, access to the farm facilities, and shared expertise. Families participating in the program pay a fee that covers registration and tuition and includes all art, science, and garden supplies, garden tools, weekly harvested produce, and an end-of-summer harvest party. Expenses include staff salaries, materials, supplies, and insurance fees. After expenses are deducted from the total program fees, any profit is split between the museum and the farm.

Classes are held at Coonamessett Farm, with exclusive use of its educational center during class time (including tables, chairs, and a sink). The children have an entire farm row, approximately 4 feet by 75 feet, for their class garden. Garden tools are supplied for each class (10 each of trowels, garden forks, child-size rakes and hoes, watering cans, small weeding buckets, and kneeling pads, plus two each of the above in adult sizes for teachers). Each child is encouraged to bring his or her own pair of garden gloves and a basket or bucket for harvesting. Additional garden supplies and materials (trellis, compost, fertilizer, wheelbarrow, seeds and plants, etc.) are provided as necessary, as are all art and science materials required. The children are each given a personal farm and garden journal (a bound blank book) to work on, adding their own unique thoughts and artwork over the course of the summer. These journals (with photographs from the session inserted by the teacher as a surprise) become treasured keepsakes of the children's *Little Sprouts* experience.

Three *Little Sprouts* classes are offered on each of two days (six classes total), limited to 10 children each and with age-appropriate peer groups. A variety of class times are available, some in the morning and some in the afternoon, avoiding the hottest portion of the day. Classes meet weekly for one and a half hours—enough time to accomplish program goals without exhausting the children. Meeting once a week fosters a sense of magic and anticipation, as many changes occur in the garden over the course of the week; meeting more often could transform spirited and fun garden work into garden chores and boredom!

Class Content

Little Sprouts classes focus on a different farm or garden theme each week (for example, seed development and plant parts, composting, beneficial insects, weather, natural fibers, farm animals). A typical class will begin with a discussion of the theme, including supporting activities (games, hands-on experience, visual aids). There is always a related arts and crafts project, either individual (vegetable prints, painted birdhouses, bug houses) or group (creating scarecrows, building fairy houses, painting large pots for herbs). Depending on the daily theme, there may be a science project (building a worm farm, hatching butterflies, soil testing, using magnifying glasses to examine insects, incubating an egg). Each class includes work in the garden—planting, weeding, watering, fertilizing, and harvesting—with frequent breaks for cool water (supplied at each class).

Classes finish with a walk on the farm to feed the chickens, visit the farm animals, and explore what's happening in the fields and greenhouses. The children bring their harvest baskets to gather new and different vegetables, herbs, and berries to taste and share with their families: turnips, beets, chard, raspberries, cabbage, cilantro—whatever is in season. All of the children promise to try and taste everything that they carry home in their baskets! This encourages them and their families to try new foods and strengthens awareness of locally grown food. All produce harvested from the *Little Sprouts* garden is shared among the children. Handouts (recipes, articles of interest, further experiments or craft ideas) are distributed to parents, encouraging continued learning and family support. Weekly follow-up emails to parents ensure good communication about the previous week's class, upcoming class plans, farm events, and other essential or interesting information.

Replication Tips

A program modeled on *Little Sprouts* could be replicated or adapted at a museum of any size. Gardens, whether in-ground or raised bed, could be built and maintained on the premises. Techniques such as organic gardening methods and composting could be taught to the children. Garden-related science experiments and arts and crafts could be offered, and support information, including recipes and other handouts, could be made available to families. Knowledgeable members of the community—master gardeners, beekeepers, farmers, artisans, and craftspeople—could add their hands-on experience and expertise to the curriculum, or field trips for the children could be arranged. Most desirable would be the opportunity to establish a working partnership with a local farm, nursery, or community garden such as Coonamessett Farm.

Conclusion

What if joyful children skip down the hill toward their teacher each week, baskets in hand, calling "What are we picking today? Can we water the garden? Has the baby donkey been born yet?" *Little Sprouts* children do, and the program has been successful primarily because of the unique opportunity for the museum to partner with a real working farm within the community. Coonamessett Farm shares many of the museum's goals for healthy practices, encouraging families to experience nature on the farm and to eat healthy locally grown foods. The Cape Cod Children's Museum is able to offer a wonderfully exciting, creative, and special opportunity for children through its *Little Sprouts* program. The museum team encourages other museums to seek out and establish similar partnerships in their own communities.

Food and Scientific Illiteracy

Mary L. Nucci and William K. Hallman

Abstract

Food consumption choices are laden with meaning beyond issues of health or nutrition. Unfortunately, these choices are often driven by cultural constructs obtained from popular culture or word of mouth. Because food is ubiquitous, imbedded in our cultural milieu, and absolutely essential to life, it is important to consider the potential variables that confound the dissemination of scientific information about food issues. The results of a decade-worth of multiple audience studies examining public perceptions about the food/health linkage of food and new food technologies demonstrate that scientific illiteracy and confusion are often key to consumers' ability to evaluate and make decisions about food choices. Science centers' and museums' expertise in communicating science to multiple audiences could play an important role in addressing scientific illiteracy about food.

About the authors

Mary L. Nucci (PhD) is a Research Assistant Professor in the Department of Human Ecology at Rutgers, the State University of New Jersey. Her research addresses issues of perception of science and science communication in film, mass media, and museums. She served as Director of the Health Floor at Liberty Science Center. William K. Hallman (PhD) is the Director of the Food Policy Institute, and Professor and Chair of the Department of Human Ecology at Rutgers. His research examines perceptions of controversial issues concerning food, health, and the environment, including food safety risks, the use of nanotechnology in food, and public understanding of food health claims.

Museums & Social Issues, Volume 7, Number 1, Spring 2012, pp. 59–69.

Consumers' perceptions of new food technologies are often different from those of other product technologies (Gaskell, Allum, & Stares, 2003; Gaskell, Ten Eyck, Jackson, & Veltri, 2005). In part, this is because food carries distinct religious, symbolic, and cultural meanings. People use food choices to represent and communicate who they are as individuals (Sadalla & Burroughs, 1981), their roles in society, or to express their political or ideological beliefs. Feasting, fasting, ritual preparation, and taboos or restrictions regarding the touching or eating of certain foods play crucial roles in religious and cultural practices and identities (Bynum, 1985; Douglas, 1966, 1972; Fiddes, 1994; Levi-Strauss, 1966, 1970). Giving food to or sharing food with others is considered crucial to creating and maintaining bonds between people (Miller, Rozin, & Fiske, 1998).

In studies examining consumer perceptions of new food technologies, perceived costs, and benefits (Frewer, Scholderer & Lambert, 2003; Ronteltap, van Trijp, Renes, & Frewer, 2007), the technology used (Lahteenmaki, Lyly, & Urala, 2007), the manufacturing process involved (Caporale & Monteleone, 2004), and issues of morality, democracy, and uncertainty (Brown & Ping, 2003; Hallman, Adelaja, Schilling, & Lang, 2002; Siegrist, 2000) have all been shown to be major factors in determining consumer acceptance. Critically, however, the public perception of new food technologies is often influenced by the mental models consumers have about new technology. For example, the lack of consumer acceptance of food irradiation technology is often blamed, in part, on the public's inability to separate the concept of irradiation from that of radiation. The negative affective responses many have towards radiation, and specifically towards the thought of food potentially contaminated by radiation, lead many consumers to reject the idea of irradiated foods (Resurreccion, Galvez, Fletcher, & Misra, 1995). Similarly, although the use of carbon monoxide in modified atmosphere meat and seafood packaging is recognized as safe by the FDA, many consumers perceive this practice as unacceptable not only as it might mask food spoilage (Boyle, 2006; Weiss, 2006), but also because of their knowledge that carbon monoxide is a poisonous and deadly gas (Health Sciences Institute, 2012).

Knowledge in Public Perceptions of Food Issues

In a series of audience studies over the last 15 years, we have examined public perceptions of a variety of food-related issues, including genetic modification (GM), animal cloning, food safety, health-related food claims, and nanotechnology. In 2004, when presented with stories about GM food taken from the media, the majority of those questioned found every story to be somewhat believable. This included two stories relating false information that had been circulated by the media and the internet: that people had allergic reactions to GM foods, and that a large fast-food chain was selling chicken products "so altered by genetic modification that they can't be called 'chicken' anymore" (Hallman, Hebden, Cuite, Aquino, & Lang, 2004, p. 6).

When asked what ideas or concepts came to mind when they heard the terms genetic modification, genetic engineering, or biotechnology, those questioned said that the term "genetic modification" yielded images of Frankenstein, test-tube babies, mutants or monsters; "genetic engineering" evoked references to sheep, lambs, or names that rhymed with Dolly, the first cloned sheep (Polly, Molly, Golly); and "biotechnology" was associated with new medicines, new foods, the future, or progress. Of all the terms, biotechnology was linked most to science terms, such as test-tubes, laboratories, DNA or chemicals (Hallman, Adelaja, Schilling, & Lang, 2002).

When opinion leaders were asked about their understanding of animal cloning, many were unable to distinguish between cloning and genetic modification. Initial responses focused more on whether they (or others) thought it was a good or bad idea rather than describing what cloning is and how it is accomplished. In spite of their lack of knowledge about the science, they were more interested in questions such as who is doing cloning, what are the goals, what is the current status of the research, are the cloned animals normal, who is regulating the technology, and is the technology safe, and not on the science behind animal cloning (Hallman & Condry, 2006).

It was shown that consumers often don't have the objective knowledge about food pathogens and symptoms of foodborne illness to make appropriate decisions about food safety (Onyango, Miljkovic, Hallman, Nganje, Condry, & Cuite, 2007). Research suggested that audiences needed guided information about food safety that was relevant to their needs, concerns, and responsibilities, and that more efforts needed to be directed toward public education and outreach efforts on issues of food safety that would target younger consumers, those with lower levels of education, and unmarried individuals who were less likely to be aware of food recalls (Hallman, Cuite, & Hooker, 2009). Because of varying levels of education and experience, audiences had greater or lesser abilities to understand and put into practice the information or ideas presented in food safety communications; messages needed to be constructed to take this into account (Hallman, 2008).

Consumers questioned about health claims on food were often confused by the content of the claim. In some cases, they said they would go against FDA recommendations if they had other evidence. Incorrect knowledge about health claims was not uncommon, such as assuming that canola oil was toxic as it was related to the chemical weapon mustard gas;[1] or a lack of information about a health claim which is interpreted as the claim possibly being dangerous ("If I don't know what it is, it can't be effective. It could be poison."). Concerns about the amount of information ("Personally, if there is a lot of information, I skip it.") or the language used (layman's language versus scientific terms) would lead consumers to avoid foods with health benefits.

In a series of interviews on food nanotechnology, very few of the participants interviewed knew anything about the technology. When asked what came to mind when they heard the word 'nanotechnology,' participants mentioned computers, iPods, chips, junk drives, or lasers; medical therapies such as miniature cameras for in vitro examination and monitoring or repairing human cells; and popular culture such as in the tv show *Mork and Mindy* (the character Mork used the phrase "nanu nanu" to say hello), *James Bond*, and *Stargate* (Nucci & Hallman, 2012).

Many knew that the term nanotechnology was somehow linked to concepts of size: "Because I just think of something little when you say 'nano.' I think my kids have something that's 'nano' and its small." "Well, I don't know much about it, but 'nano' usually means something small." "The smaller it is, the better." "Very small but intelligent." However, no participant was able to describe the key attributes of nanotechnology identified in most authoritative definitions;[2] that is, the ability to understand and manipulate matter at the nanoscale, and the capability to generate and make use of the novel properties of materials at the molecular level (Nucci & Hallman, 2012).

Participants struggled to come up with a linkage between nanotechnology and food. Several mentioned processed, engineered, or efficient food as an outcome of using nanotechnology. Others felt that the use of nanotechnology would be associated with healthier foods, new or novel cooking technologies, microwaves or cooking equipment, or improvements in agricultural production through increased yield, hybridization of plants or animals, prevention of illness in animals, or replacement of pesticides.

Even when given the opportunity to read about nanotechnology in the National Nanotechnology Initiative (NNI) brochure *Nanotechnology: Big Things from a Tiny World* (National Nanotechnology Initiative, 2011b), participants were still not able to comfortably describe what nanotechnology was or its application to food. Participants linked nanotechnology to food through time and size concepts such as growing food faster or easier, growing bigger fruits and vegetables, or increasing yield; others linked nanotechnology to food through food engineering (taste/color/quality and creating new foods), production of healthier food, new and improved cooking technologies, and packaging (Nucci & Hallman, 2012).

Food Communication: Museums at the Table

Over the past decade our research has consistently demonstrated that a lack of familiarity—knowledge and mis-knowledge—plays an important role in public perceptions and attitudes about food decisions and that the consumer may often be laboring under false knowledge or false constructs in decision making. For most Americans, television is the primary source of information for science and technology (National Science Board, 2012) as well as food and nutrition (American Dietetic Association, 2002; Hoban & Kendall, 1993; International Food Information Council (IFIC), 2005; Verbeke, 2005). However, a demonstrated lack of coverage and content in television information about science (Nucci, Cuite, & Hallman, 2009; Nucci & Kubey, 2007; Project for Excellence in Journalism, 2007[3]) begs the question: Is there a better way to disseminate information about food? The answer may lie in what our research has shown and what museums do well.

Our research has pointed out that relevancy, rhetoric, linkage to false constructs ("irrational thinking"; Valdecasas & Correas, 2010), the need to tailor messages to specific audiences, and a range of educational levels are all key to learning about food. Differences in age, education, gender (Hallman et al., 2003), ethnicity, religion, and trust in scientists, corporations, and government (Hallman et al., 2002; Siegrist, 1999, 2000) are all important factors in decision-making about science. Whether it is the lack of knowledge or irrational knowledge, such as conflating mustard gas with canola oil or "nanu nanu" with nanotechnology, heuristics related to other technologies or other knowledges must be carefully considered. As in the case with food irradiation, public opinion can as easily be based on objective science as on negative constructs; but it is less easily displaced when science is considered difficult or confusing.

Informal science learning programs are characterized by their consideration of all of these factors (relevancy, language, content, diversity, educational background), as well as multiple levels of engagement (physical, emotional, cognitive), building upon prior knowledge, and self-guided learning (Fenichel & Schweingruber, 2010). Museums are good at interaction, relevancy, context, and audience, and can provide a safe place to interact and question. With the growing trend to their contextualizing science in society, museums can consider the range of ethical, moral, environmental, and social questions about science. It has been shown that the learning experiences in informal environments are "believed to lead to further inquiry, enjoyment and a sense that science learning can be personally relevant and rewarding" (National Research Council, 2009, p. 11). Inviting museums to the food table could prove to address the deficiencies in communicating science fact about food and food issues, driven as they are by a "complex decision-making calculus" (Currall et al., 2006, p. 154) of knowledge and mis-knowledge.

Notes

1. Canola oil comes from either the rapeseed or mustard plant. Mustard gas, so-called because of its yellow color and an aroma like mustard, is sulfur mustard (Canola Council of Canada, 2007). See also www.snopes.com/medical/toxins/canola.asp
2. The Center for Responsible Nanotechnlogy (2008) describes nanotechnology in terms of engineering at the molecular scale. The National Nanotechnology Initiative (2011a) defines nanotechnology in terms of size impacting function and application. The Food and Drug Administration (2010) characterizes nanotechnology as a process of creation and manipulation at the nanoscale resulting in materials with different properties.
3. In 2007, science stories accounted for only 1% of the total news time on the morning news television network shows and only 2% of news time on the evening television network news shows (Project for Excellence in Journalism, 2007).

Acknowledgments

Research described here was funded by Grant 2008-01415 to the_Food Policy Institute, Rutgers, the State University of New Jersey, from the Cooperative State Research, Education, and Extension Service of the United States Department of Agriculture (USDA): *Food Nanotechnology: Understanding the Parameters of Consumer Acceptance*, Dr. William K. Hallman, principal investigator; Grant 2002-52100-11203 from the U.S. Department of Agriculture (USDA), under the Initiative for the Future of Agricultural Food Systems: *Evaluating Consumer Acceptance of Food Biotechnology in the United States*, Dr. William K. Hallman, principal investigator; and Grant 66487 from the Robert Wood

Johnson Foundation: *The Diet-Health Nexus: Communicating Emerging Evidence*, Dr. William K. Hallman, principal investigator. The opinions expressed are those of the authors and do not necessarily reflect official positions or policies of the USDA, the New Jersey Agricultural Experiment Station, the Robert Wood Johnson Foundation, or the Food Policy Institute, Rutgers, the State University of New Jersey.

References

Boyle, T. (2006). *Groups protest use of carbon monoxide in meat packaging.* Accessed from www.usatoday.com/news/health/2006-02-21-carbon-monoxide-meat_x.htm

Bynum, C. W. (1985). Fast, feast, & flesh: The religious significance of food to medieval women. *Representations, 11*, 1–25.

Brown, J. L., & Ping, Y. (2003). Consumer perception of risk associated with eating genetically engineered (GE) soybeans is less in the presence of a perceived consumer benefit. *Journal of the American Dietetic Association, 103*(2), 208–214.

Canola Council of Canada. (2007). What is canola oil? Accessed from canolainfo.org/canola/index.php

Caporale, G., & Monteleone, E. (2004). Influence of information about manufacturing process on beer acceptability. *Food Quality and Preference, 15*, 271–278.

Center for Responsible Nanotechnology. (2008). *What is nanotechnology?* Accessed from www.crnano.org/whatis.htm

Currall, S. C., King, E. B., Lane, N., Madera, J., & Turner, S. (2006). What drives public acceptance of nanotechnology? *Nature Nanotechnology, 1*, 153–155.

Douglas, M. (1966). *Purity and danger.* London: Routledge.

Douglas, M. (1972). Deciphering a meal. *Daedalus, 10*, 61–81.

Fenichel, M., & Schweingruber, H. A. (2010). *Surrounded by science: Learning science in informal environments.* Board on Science Education, Center for Education, Division of Behavioral and Social Sciences and Education. Washington, DC: The National Academies Press.

Fiddes, N. (1994). Social aspects of meat eating. *Proceedings of the Nutrition Society, 53*(2), 271–279.

Food and Drug Administration. (2010). *Nanotechnology.* Accessed from www.fda.gov/ScienceResearch/SpecialTopics/Nanotechnology/default.htm

Frewer, L. Scholderer, J., & Lambert, N. (2003). Consumer acceptance of functional foods: Issues for the future. *British Food Journal, 105*, 714–731.

Gaskell, G., Allum, N., & Stares, S. (2003). *Europeans and biotechnology in 2002: Eurobarometer 58.0.* Brussels: European Commission.

Gaskell, G., Ten Eyck, T., Jackson, J., & Veltri, G. (2005). Imagining nanotechnology: Cultural support for technological innovation in Europe and the United States. *Public Understanding of Science, 14*(1), 81–90.

Hallman, W. K. (2008). Communicating about microbial risks in foods. In D. W. Schaffner (Ed.), *Microbial risk analysis of foods* (pp. 205–262). Washington, D C: American Society for Microbiology Press.

Hallman, W. K., Adelaja, A. O., Schilling, B. J., & Lang, J. (2002). Public perceptions of genetically modified foods: Americans know not what they eat. (Food Policy Institute Report No. RR-0302-001). New Brunswick: Rutgers, the State University of New Jersey, Food Policy Institute.

Hallman, W.K., & Condry, S. C. (2006). *Public opinion and media coverage of animal cloning and the food supply. Executive summary.* Accessed from *Food Policy Institute, Rutgers, the State University of New Jersey,* New Brunswick, NJ. FPI Research Report RR-1106-011.

Hallman, W. K., Cuite, C. L., & Hooker, N. H. (2009). Consumer Responses to Food Recalls: 2008 National Survey Report. (Publication number RR-0109-018). New Brunswick: Rutgers, the State University of New Jersey, Food Policy Institute.

Hallman, W. K., Hebden, W., Aquino, H., Cuite, C., & Lang, J. (2003). Public perceptions of genetically modified foods: A national study of American knowledge and opinion. Food Policy Institute Report RR-1003-004.

Hallman, W. K., Hebden, W. C., Cuite, C. L., Aquino, H. L., & Lang, J. T. (2004). Americans and GM food: Knowledge, opinion & interest in 2004. (Food Policy Institute Report No. RR-1104-007). New Brunswick: Rutgers, the State University of New Jersey, Food Policy Institute.

Health Sciences Institute. (2012). *Carbon monoxide as a meat preservative.* Accessed from hsionline.com/2006/09/05/carbon-monoxide-as-a-meat-preservative/

Hoban, T. J., & Kendall, P. A. (1993). *Consumer attitudes about food biotechnology.* Raleigh: North Carolina Cooperative Extension Service.

IFIC (International Food Information Council). (2005). Food for thought VI. Executive Summary. Retrieved from www.foodinsight.org/Content/3651/ExecSummaryFFTVI.pdf

Lahteenmaki, L., Lyly, M., & Urala, N. (2007). Consumer attitudes towards functional foods. In L. Frewer & H. van Trijp (Eds.), *Understanding consumers of food products.* Cambridge, UK: Woodhead.

Levi-Strauss, C. (1966). The culinary triangle. *New Society, 166,* 937–940.

Levi-Strauss, C. (1970). *The raw and the cooked.* London: Cape.

Miller, L., Rozin, P., & Fiske, A. P. (1998). Food sharing and feeding another person suggest intimacy; Two studies of American college students. *European Journal of Social Psychology, 28,* 423–436.

National Nanotechnology Initiative. (2011a). What is nanotechnology? National Nanotechnology Initiative website. Accessed from www.nano.gov/nanotech-101/what

National Nanotechnology Initiative. (2011b). *Nanotechnology: Big things from a tiny world.* Accessed from www.nano.gov/node/240

National Research Council. (2009). *Learning science in informal environments: People, places, and pursuits.* Committee on Learning Science in Informal Environments. P. Bell, B. Lewenstein, A. W. Shouse, & M. A. Feder, (Eds.) Board on Science Education, Center for Education. Division of Behavioral and Social Sciences and Education. Washington, DC: The National Academies Press.

National Science Board. (2012). *Science and engineering indicators 2012.* Accessed from www.nsf.gov/statistics/seind12/start.htm

Nucci, M. L., Cuite, C. L., & Hallman, W. K. (2009). When good food goes bad: Television network news and the spinach outbreak of 2006. *Science Communication, 31*(2), 238–265

Nucci, M.L., & Hallman, W.K. (2012). Mork and Mindy, canola oil and mustard gas: The dilemma of scientific illiteracy in decisions about food and health. J. Goodwin (Ed.), *Between scientists and citizens: Proceedings of a conference at Iowa State University, June 1-2, 2012* (pp. 307–314).

Nucci, M.L., & Kubey, R. (2007). "We begin tonight with fruits and vegetables": Genetically modified (GM) food on the evening news 1980–2003. *Science Communication, 29*: 147–176.

Onyango, B., Miljkovic, D., Hallman, W., Nganje, W., Condry, S., & Cuite, C. (2007, August). Food recalls and food safety perceptions: The September 2006 Spinach Recall Case. Paper presented at the annual joint meetings of the AAEA, WAEA and CAES, Portland, OR.

Project for Excellence in Journalism. (2007). *The state of the news media 2007: An annual report on American journalism.* Accessed from www.stateofthenewsmedia.org/2007/

Resurreccion, A. V. A., Galvez, F. C. F., Fletcher, S. M., & Misra, S. K. (1995). Consumer attitudes toward irradiated food: Results of a new study. *Journal of Food Protection, 58*(2), 193–196.

Sadalla, E. K., & Burroughs, W. J. (1981). Profiles in eating. *Psychology Today, 15*(10), 51–57.

Siegrist, M. (1999). A causal model explaining the perception and acceptance of gene technology. *Journal of Applied Social Psychology, 29*(10), 2093–2106.

Siegrist, M. (2000). The influence of trust and perceptions of risks and benefits on the acceptance of gene technology. *Risk Analysis, 20*(2), 195–204.

Valdecasas, A.G., & Correas, A.M. (2010). Science literacy and natural history museums. *Journal of Bioscience, 35*, 507–514.

Verbeke, W. (2005). Agriculture and the food industry in the information age. *European Review of Agricultural Economics, 32*, 347–368.

Weiss, R. (2006, October 19). Religion a prominent cloned-food issue. *The Washington Post*, p. A9.

A Jar of Pickles, a Glass of Tea, a Bowl of Borscht

Conversations in a Changing Ukraine

Linda Norris

Abstract

Using the Pickle Project as a case study, this article examines how conversations about food can effectively engage audiences of all types in thoughtful discussions about not solely food, but larger issues as well. Drawing on our experience with this project, I analyze the project's fieldwork and public conversations in Ukraine. Based on that work, I explore lessons learned and how they might apply to museums interested in exploring food as a focus for their work.

About the author

Linda Norris is an independent museum professional working to create compelling narratives, connect audiences and museums, and encourage the development of new approaches to museum work. She is the author of the widely read blog, *The Uncataloged Museum* (http://uncatalogedmuseum.blogspot.com), and was a Fulbright Scholar to Ukraine in 2009 and 2010.

Museums & Social Issues, Volume 7, Number 1, Spring 2012, pp. 71–82.

Natalia Stryamets shares a dish in her family home, 2011. *Photo by author.*

A bowl of borscht, a root cellar full of jars of pickled cucumbers and tomatoes, a bag of freshly foraged mushrooms, a woman selling potatoes and cabbage on a busy wintry street, a cup of tea. Observing the adaptability, seasonality, and self-sufficiency of Ukrainian food practices, the Pickle Project (pickleproject.blogspot.com) was founded on the idea that these simple foods reflect both the cultural and natural environments and are worth sharing as Western audiences ponder ways to build sustainability in their food systems.

Ukraine is an ancient culture but a young nation. Various regions of Ukraine have been part of the Russian Empire, the Austro-Hungarian Empire, the Ottoman Empire and, of course, most recently, the Soviet Union. It was once known as the Breadbasket of Europe. Despite the country's incredibly rich fertile black soil, throughout the 20th century, Ukrainians knew times of great hunger and starvation, most notably Holodomor, the Great Famine of 1932–33 (an artificial famine created by Stalin), and throughout the fighting of World War II.[1] The Chernobyl nuclear disaster brought ongoing concerns about food and nuclear safety. With independence in 1991, came extraordinary change, free markets, new opportunities, and a great deal of uncertainty. Today, Ukraine's current president has worked to roll back some of the freedoms garnered over the last 20 years and many Ukrainians fear a return to the old authoritarian ways.

Ukraine is geographically diverse—from the Carpathian Mountains in the West, to the steppes of Central and Eastern Ukraine, to the Mediterranean-like landscape of Crimea. It is culturally diverse as well; in additional to ethnic Ukrainians and Russians, there are small populations of ethnic minorities like the Hutsul, Lempko, and Boiko in the Carpathians. Crimean Tatars continue to return to their Crimean homeland, after forced eviction to Central Asia under the Soviet regime. There is a growing Jewish community, returning to places that were once centers of Jewish culture and life before the Second World War. Ukraine is also seeing new populations of Uzbeks, Byelorussians, Moldavians, and others coming to the country, looking for fresh opportunities.

Anna Khvyl and her mother at the Bulgakov Pickle Project Conversation, 2011.

Students at the Pickle Project Conversation in Donetsk, 2011.

Sarah Crow and I co-founded the Pickle Project 2009. I originally went to Kyiv, Ukraine, in January 2009 to spend four months as a United States Fulbright Scholar, teaching museum studies and working directly with museums. My co-founder, Sarah Crow, arrived earlier that fall for a 10-month period, also as a Fulbright Scholar, to research issues associated with rural development and forestry in Western Ukraine. Separately, we found the link between the food and culture of Ukraine complicated and complex, reflecting a rapidly changing society. Upon our return to the United States, a chance conversation led us to develop the Pickle Project blog as a way of further considering those issues and sharing them with a broader audience.

In Ukrainian museums (the vast majority of which are government museums), there were almost no museum educators; the scientists (what Americans think of as curators or subject matter specialists) focused on research, and many Ukrainians I met felt that museums had little relevance to them. I brought my experience in developing projects that engage communities to conversations and workshops with Ukrainian museum colleagues, which in turn enhanced our thinking about the Pickle Project. Sarah's conservation and governance experiences and her Ukrainian colleagues equally helped shape her thinking about issues of food, development, and sustainability. This multi-disciplinary approach has been a critical element of the Pickle Project.

Designing Community Based Conversations Around Food

In October 2011, with the support of the Trust for Mutual Understanding, we returned to Ukraine with two other Americans, Caleb Zigas of La Cocina, a San Francisco non-profit organization that works with immigrant food entrepreneurs, and Minnesota cheese maker Rueben Nilsson, to co-convene a series of public conversations about food in four Ukrainian cities. We had very different partners in each city: a museum, a cultural management organization, a non-governmental agency that coordinates the Model UN and other international topics, and an arts organization that works primarily with young people. To respond to local context and culture, we encouraged each organization to develop an event that met their community's needs. As a result, each conversation was very different. The four Pickle Project Conversations reflect how organizational partners, social media, time of day, and even venue make a difference in the ways in which community members come together and the form a conversation can take.

The Arc of Dialogue method, used by many sites in the International Coalition of Historic Sites network and the National Park Service (2012), was useful in crafting the conversation plans. We also agreed from the start, among ourselves and with our project partners, that this was an experimental process. As a group, we were ready to learn and adapt as we went along.

The overall plan was a very brief (and it got briefer over time) introduction to the project, and then two short presentations—one by Linda and one by Caleb—which used personal experiences to shape a discussion question. In two smaller groups, participants discussed those questions. Next, we came back together for framing questions from Rueben and Sarah, returning to small groups for more discussion. The event concluded with the full group sharing final comments and questions. We began with the simplest questions that drew on personal memories about food, then moved to questions about food and the economy, on to the science of food, and ended with questions about sustainability and the future of food.

A. Bulgakov Museum, Kyiv

The Bulgakov Museum in Kyiv, Ukraine's capital, is the former home of author Mikhail Bulgakov, best known to millions as the author of *The Master and Margarita.* It's a small house museum but one of the most inventive museums in Kyiv. The museum has done other food-related events in the past, such as celebrating the grapes from their arbor out back with an evening of food, wine, and music. The staff at the Bulgakov still view the building as a home and are deeply committed to a homelike atmosphere for everyone. The event was promoted through the museum, but also through social media such as Facebook and Live Journal (a Russian language social networking site). We attended the first-ever Kyiv organic food producers market the day before, and several organic entrepreneurs took us up on our invitation to join the conversation. The crowd was a lively mix that included diplomats and dairy farmers, rural development specialists, municipal managers, grandmas, college students, and teenagers. The spaces are cozy at the Bulgakov, and this effect was enhanced as the director and deputy director served as hosts, passing around homely but great-tasting kasha, paired with pickles brought by a participant, and other snacks. A little vodka, of course, is the traditional accompaniment. These combined atmospheric elements set the stage for good conversations among people who had never met one another before.

B. Eko-Art, Donetsk

On a stormy night in Donetsk, an industrial center of Eastern Ukraine, we hurried down a gusty street, clutching our umbrellas and leaping over ankle-deep streams at intersections, to arrive at our second Pickle Project conversation, at a high school. "Welcome to Potluck" the chalkboard read. Valentyna Sahnenko, director of Eko-Art, and her colleagues had marshaled an enthusiastic group of students and their teacher and viewed the conversation as an extension of their ongoing work with young people. We were thrilled to see that students had all brought home-cooked food to share with the group. This teenage audience was one of the liveliest, and they had many questions for us. Those questions spanned not only the cultural gap, but also a generational one, with questions about what teenagers eat, how old are you when you go out on dates, and if young people have more freedom in the United States. This conversation particularly helped to frame more questions about the ways that adolescents perceive food in their own and other cultures.

C. PIC the Project for Intercultural Cooperation, Odessa

In Odessa, on the Black Sea, our conversation was held in a formal space at the Bulgarian Culture Centre. Because of its history as a port, this city is one of the most diverse places in Ukraine, and its citizens are proud of that diversity. Hannah Shelest, Director of PIC, the Project for Intercultural Cooperation, our organizing partner, made a connection with the head of the local Department for National Minorities. They invited representatives from the many nationalities in Odessa. Participants were older in age and were generally leaders of their local cultural organization. Consequently, this conversation was framed more around issues of ethnic identity, knowledge transmission, and memory rather than issues of economy and sustainability.

D. Centre for Cultural Management, L'viv

L'viv, in Western Ukraine, is considered one of Ukraine's intellectual centers and a center of Ukrainian nationalism. Our partner, the Centre for Cultural Management, trains cultural managers and undertakes projects both in L'viv and throughout the nation. This conversation was held at Ye Bookstore, attracting both those who came specifically for the event and those who dropped into the conversation while browsing. As in Kyiv, the group was diverse in terms of both age and gender. The discussions were equally wide-ranging, from how the tax structure can support farmers to why young Ukrainians no longer make borscht but would rather make sushi!

At each location we invited participants to share their thoughts with Post-it notes and markers on a number of issues—What makes food healthy? What's your favorite food? This provided a casual way for participants to begin thinking about the connections between daily food practices, culture, economy, and landscape. It also provided a way for strangers to engage in conversation, not a normal practice in Ukraine.

Our experiences reinforced elements that anyone who does museum programs already knows: the space arrangement matters; the composition of an audience can completely change a program's direction; and flexibility is key. And, of course, any event is better with food.

How Can Museums Learn from the Pickle Project?

Informal Fieldwork Is Okay

Community-based projects often go unstarted because there is not enough money or time for research or fieldwork. This project began through day-to-day observations of the places we were living and the people we knew—the food for sale on the street, served at family meals, or grown in gardens. Because the production of food is an everyday occurrence, fieldwork and connection building can happen at nearly any time and in any place. A museum's intent may be to make connections, to understand a local community, and to encourage conversation. Those are things that can happen in informal ways.

Food Topics Stimulate Highly Accessible, Passionate Conversation

Food has so many access points and touches our lives in a myriad of ways. It is of both emotional and pragmatic consequence. A memory of varenyky, a stuffed Ukrainian dumpling, served under the dappled light of pear trees; a recipe for plov, a rice pilaf, carried back from Central Asia by a Crimean Tatar, returning to the homeland; the citrus taste of sea buckthorn, harvested in dark boreal forests. Those sensual emotional consequences colored our conversations. But they were accompanied by talk about

Participants consider the future of food and villages, 2011.

larger issues. What would you do if you were minister of agriculture? Who can you trust to make your food safe? What effect will genetic modified foods have on us? And what, if anything, "tasty" really means in a land that's known great scarcity. Almost everyone cares about food—and is passionate about sharing his or her own traditions, experiences, and perspectives.

Food Opens Conversational Doors to Bigger Issues

Framing the dialogue from the personal to the global made it possible to broach larger issues and connect them to daily life. The conversations made people think that perhaps it was possible and important to continue talking about food, to consider how to hold a government responsible, or how to communicate their ideas to others. Open conversations are critical to the functioning of a civil society. But in societies where conversations have been closed, the door can open through an accessible topic like food.

Food Encourages Curiosity and Challenges Stereotypes

Travel in Ukraine is challenging and the country is diverse with differences exacerbated by complex histories, divergent interests, and political agendas. In these conversations, participants wanted to know what people in other parts of the country thought. Each event provided a chance for people to ask questions of people from other backgrounds that they, perhaps, would not or could not ask in other settings. By structuring the conversations to begin with personal, relatable stories, we set the stage for questions. From questions and answers about food, conversations moved to greater understandings of cultural and religious traditions, shared in ways that reflected living traditions, rather than the static presentation of a museum exhibition.

Audiences were very curious about American food, which they know from movies, television, and the fast food outlets found in larger Ukrainian cities. As we explained our own family traditions, local food movements, ethnic restaurants, and other aspects of the contemporary American food scene, we could address and contextualize stereotypical views and media images.

Ukrainian independence allowed for the introduction of a range of new perspectives from outside the Soviet Union. But the old Soviet method of conveying information still holds sway in many settings. A designated "expert" stands up, reads a paper at

A family meal in Kyiv, 2011.

full speed, and sits down. No questions are asked and no interactions are made. One of our goals was to present an alternative to this approach. Because we and, more notably, our local partners were willing to take risks with format and technique, we gained significant rewards. Ihor Savchuk, director of the Centre for Cultural Management, wrote:

> The event was really innovative and fresh, and the participants loved the loose format of the conversation where they had enough space for their personal stories and interpretations.…[I]t was an inspiring meeting in the city and people loved it. We would like to be associated with the things people love.

In changing American communities, where the demographics may be very different than the ones in play when today's museums were founded, we are finding new ways to connect with communities. Shared authority—finding space for personal stories and interpretations—provides the opportunity for museums to make deeper, more substantive connections with their communities. Programs and exhibits shared around food, crowd-sourced around food traditions and new ideas about sustainability, are just one compelling way to make those connections. This curiosity about food and food differences is the same in the United States. It's not surprising that Reach Advisors (Wilkening, 2011) found that more than 50% of museum visitors have an explicit interest in food. Museum visitors are also curious about food in many cultural contexts, so a museum undertaking a food related project may find ready audiences.

Food conversations can be powerful catalysts towards civic engagement. To that end, we are in the process of establishing the Pickle Project as a non-profit organization. Our mission is to promote global, cross-cultural understanding by connecting diverse communities in shared explorations of the ways in which food practices influence and reflect social, economic, and ecological conditions in rapidly changing societies. In pursuit of our goal, we will create more interactive frameworks for lively civic engagement, contributing to the democratic life of communities across the globe.

Our ambitious goals spring from the simplest experiences of asking to see a root cellar or how pickles were made, or inquiring if perhaps we could come to dinner. After one such inquiry, in a small Soviet-era flat, we crowded around a happy table with Svetlana, Vladimir, their daughter, and the neighbors. Our conversation turned to the past, to what leaders of the Soviet Union wanted their citizens to think about Americans and what American leaders wanted their citizens to think about the Soviets. Together, we laughed at the strangeness of those thoughts. Food makes us all human together.

Notes

1. For an extremely thoughtful overview of the effect of both Stalin's and Hitler's policies towards Ukraine and other nations, see Timothy Snyder, *Bloodlands: Europe Between Hitler and Stalin* (2006), New York: Basic Books.
2. For a fuller description of the conversations, refer to the relevant posts on the Pickle Project blog (pickleproject.blogspot.com).
3. For an extended discussion of museums and shared authority, see *Letting Go: Sharing Authority in a User-Generated World*, edited by Bill Adair, Benjamin Filene, and Laura Koloski (2011), Philadelphia: The Pew Center for Arts and Heritage.

References

National Park Service, Dialogue Skills Training, retrieved January 15, 2012, from www.nps.gov/nero/greatplaces/DialogueSkills.htm

Wilkening, S. (2011). Do Museums Need to Care About Foodies? American Association of Museums Center for the Future of Museums blog, futureofmuseums.blogspot.com/2011/09/do-museums-need-to-care-about-foodies.html (accessed December 29, 2011).

Art Meets Beast

A Bison Roast at MCA Denver (Colorado)

Sarah Rich and Sarah Baie

We were having lunch at Denver's equitable eatery, SAME Café, when the bison idea charged through our brainstorming session and settled itself as the centerpiece of Art Meets Beast. In fact, before the bison, there was no beast—just a seed of an event that would explore the intersection of art and food.

Bison may not seem like the natural bridge between the two, but in an era when Lady Gaga poses in a dress made of meat and butchery is an elevated form of craft; and in a state that prides itself on both its livestock industry and its wilderness, bison might just be the poster animal of Colorado's modern culinary art.

And so it was decided: We'd find a rancher who could supply a whole Colorado bison, and the roasting and butchering of the beast would be, in itself, a live installation and educational demonstration. We'd lure some of the city's best chefs to participate in the spectacle, and the community would be invited to an epic feast.

To really anchor this plan in its art museum context, the event would need some meat, so to speak. First, there would be a Mixed Taste evening, one of Museum of Contemporary Art (MCA) Denver's signature programs, bringing two speakers together, each speaking on his or her topic for 20 minutes and then taking questions and answers on both topics at the same time. For this event, the pairing would be cave painting and Buffalo Bill. And there would be an intellectual main course.

Museums & Social Issues, Volume 7, Number 1, Spring 2012, pp. 83–86.

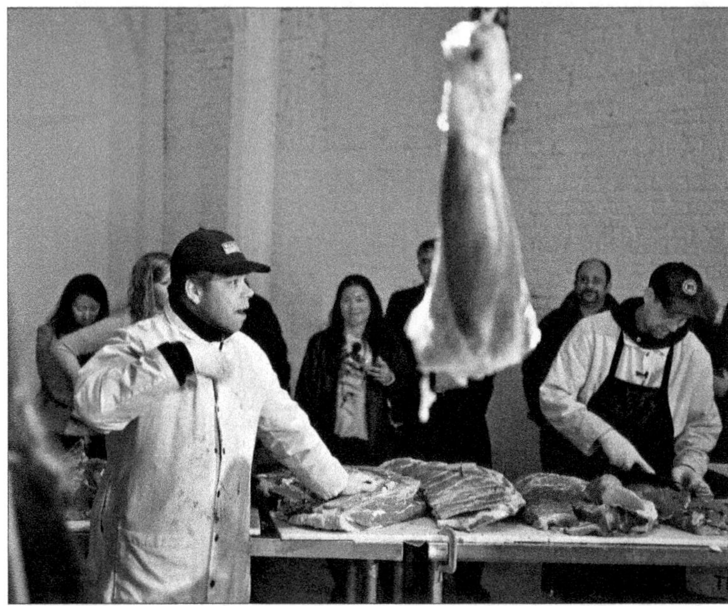

Pete Marczyk discusses animal musculature while butchering a whole bison. The meat was later distributed to chefs and used for the bison feast. *Photograph by Travis Broxton.*

For this, MCA Denver partnered with the national event series Foodprint Project to put together a live conversation about the connections between meat, design, and the city. How much can there be to say about the design of meat? Quite a lot, as it turns out.

Foodprint Project invited five local guests to sit in the hot seat for rapid-fire interviews. The discussion began at the smallest scale, examining the architecture of cattle musculature and the engineering feats of the meat industry aimed at maximizing animals' edible output. Animal scientist Keith Belk, from Colorado State University, discussed some of the high-tech tools he's developed for refining the quality of beef, including the science fictionally titled BeefCam, based on a technology previously applied to denim manufacturing. Next, neighborhood culinary ringmaster Pete Marczyck talked about the art of cutting an elegant filet and the shock and awe the shop creates among some customers by hanging whole animals in its butcher room window. Holly Arnold, owner of The Fort, described the interplay between the architecture of her legendary family restaurant and the experience of eating bison within its walls. The Fort was constructed in 1963 out of 80,000 handmade adobe bricks—a replica of the old fur-trading post, Bent's Fort. Year-round, while diners dip into an appetizer of Prairie Butter—the broiled femur marrow of a buffalo—a maintenance crew continuously patches the earthen exterior. The conversation scaled up to meat-packing with Elizabeth Dunn, associate professor of geography at UC Boulder, who described cattle as a dynamic bridge between urban life and the natural world. At the same time, she pointed out that in today's food industry, cattle often amount to little more than a machine for generating money, with efficiency trumping all. Tying it up with a macro view, Peter Decker joined the conversation—a resident rancher, historian, and probably the only former commissioner of agriculture to have played a penguin in Andy Warhol's "It's a Dog's Life." Decker debunked the myth that ranching damages land, positing that ranchers are smarter than to destroy the territory on which their cows—those bovine money machines—depend.

The Beast Roast. Rows of community tables filled the perimeter, as diners gathered for a communal feast.
Photograph by Travis Broxton.

But enough talk. It was time for the main event. The audience decamped to the Flower Garage where the great beast roast was underway. Rows of community tables filled the space, while around the perimeter some of Denver's best chefs stood ready to serve their own variations on the buffalo theme. A topical soundtrack designed by Los Angeles-based Machine Project played intermittently, bringing conversations either to a crescendo or a halt, depending on cocktail intake. An audio stampede circled the room, escalating to a deafening roar before fading out as the animals virtually disappeared over the horizon.

The beast eaters eventually filed out, stuffed, tipsy, and more intimate than ever with Colorado's wooly mascot. One had to wonder: if this was to be the first in a string of annual events merging art and food, what on earth could top the great beast roast? We've got a few ideas up our sleeves...

Sarah Rich is the digital editor for *Gastronomica: The Journal of Food and Culture* and curator of the international conversation series, "Foodprint Project." Sarah Baie is the director of programming at the Mueum of Contemporary Art Denver.

Tapas from Across and Outside the United States

The Living Cookbook

Busting Silos One Meal at a Time (Oregon)

Lexa Walsh

I moved to Portland, Oregon, in 2009 to attend the MFA program in Art and Social Practice at Portland State University. Throughout my tenure in Portland, I have collaboratively produced an assortment of cookbooks with/for/about different publics. These are catalysts for building relationships, conversation, and resource sharing. Most of these were facilitated with group meals and recipes exchanges through my inclination for being a host. I am also the Artist in Residence in the Education Department at Portland Art Museum, and I have an interest in using hospitality both in the front of the house and behind the scenes. I will discuss one of these projects, "Meal Ticket."

I am part of a lineage of artists using food in their work. Allison Knowles created fluxus scores for making giant salads. Gordon Matta-Clark started the Soho restaurant "FOOD," which was a platform for many food-related conceptual art projects. Rirkrit Tiravanija fostered hospitality in the gallery by cooking and serving pad Thai to its guests. Michael Rakowitz's "Enemy Kitchen" teaches his mother's Iraqi-Jewish recipes to willing participants, which prompts lively discussion. In Pittsburgh, Jon Rubin and Dawn Weleski started "Conflict Kitchen," serving food from countries (and cultures) the United States is in conflict with, providing a platform for cross-cultural conversation and education. Chicago's Smart Museum of Art states that

Museums & Social Issues, Volume 7, Number 1, Spring 2012, pp. 87–90.

Meal Ticket is a monthly silo-busting cross-department meal at the Portland Art Museum. *Photo courtesy of author.*

artist-orchestrated meals such as their exhibition *Feast: Radical Hospitality in Contemporary Art* "can offer a radical form of hospitality that punctures everyday experience, using food as a means to spark encounters and perceptions that aren't otherwise possible within our fast-moving and overly segmented society."

Community cookbooks have a long legacy of identifying and celebrating communities, such as museum docents, church groups, and junior leagues. They have often been used not only for fundraising, but also as collective memoirs of place and culture. They give a voice to a group of individuals, mostly women, often published for the first and only time in their lives. They carry on traditions otherwise lost, and mark the hybridization of generations of recipes. I find the cookbooks I/we have made fitting nicely in the genre of the community cookbook.

My interest in hospitality begs for a deeper investigation. Many years ago I researched and made works based on Emily Post. Post's 1922 book *Etiquette* offered advice on good taste, making etiquette accessible to many women, across financial means. My mother had a copy and adhered to it religiously. When one is the host—a woman for example—she has control in the manner of a curator. She makes aesthetic choices, selects guests, and seats them as she feels appropriate. She assembles an experience as she curates, say, a dinner party. She also has control of the act of nurturing—one of the few acts of control a woman has had, historically. She is an *experience maker.*

"Meal Ticket" is a project I am currently doing with the staff of Portland Art Museum, where I play host. The structure of "Meal Ticket" is a monthly silo-busting cross-departmental meal I cook and share with staff members. The luncheon provides an equal playing field for staff of every department, in a boardroom usually saved for trustees and upper management, in an organization that normally has a strict hierarchy. Everyone is treated to a home cooked meal, replete with seating charts and wine glasses. I seat guests to encourage cross-departmental exchange, for example seating someone from security across from someone from accounting; someone from education across from someone from events. I employ a recipe exchange as a conversation starter. There is a responsibility in this exchange system for good communication. The meals result not only in temporary lunchtime utopias, but also in access to personal stories. The recipes are not only for food but also for experiences, and they, too, are telling. The resulting cookbook is both a play on the tradition of community cookbooks and a gesture to generate relationships and conversation. As a collection, the recipes reveal our cultural references, upbringings, similarities, and differences. Recipes come with stories, about place, family, and culture. The "Meal Ticket Cookbook" was published in May 2012 with an accompanying public meal.

There are both primary and secondary audiences for these cookbooks, and there is something for each audience. Each cookbook is intended not only for the community that has created it but also for the public. The cookbooks are made as an experience. That experience can live on through the relationships built through it, through the use of the book and recipes, through the cookbook as memoir, or as an ethnographic study of the group that made it. A result of "Meal Ticket" is a notable

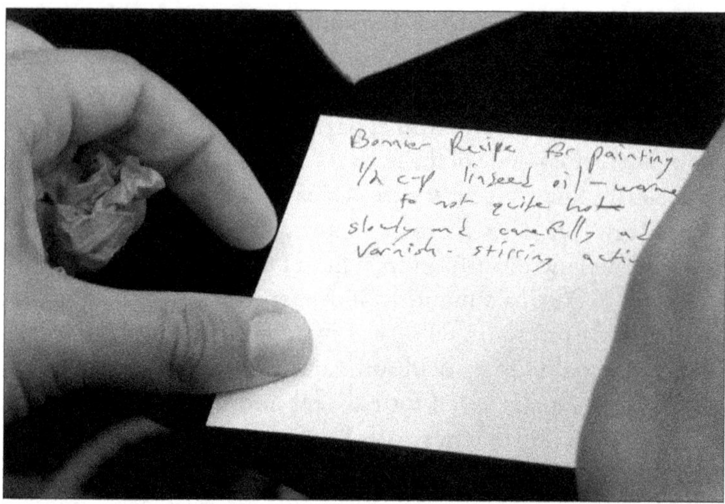

Some participants offered recipes for food, others for experiences. We learned a curator is also a painter from this recipe. *Photo courtesy of author.*

recent effort by human resources at Portland Art Museum to create more silo busting programs. The cookbooks are a residue of the experience, artworks, and tools. Those that have multiple, complex functions might read as most successful, but perhaps the longevity of the user's relationship to these experiences, each other, and this food is the evaluation of success—success that cannot yet be measured.

Lexa Walsh is an artist and musician based between Portland, Oregon, and Oakland, California. Her work engages the public in conversation, cheer, song, dance, and food. She is a recent graduate of Portland State University's Art & Social Practice MFA program and was an artist in residence at Portland Art Museum.

Tapas from Across and Outside the United States

Food: The Medium and the Message

(Kansas)

Rachel Epp Buller

Foodie, gourmet, epicure, gastronome. Carnivore, omnivore, locavore, vegetarian, vegan, ovolactarian, gluten-free, lactose-free. Our language provides us with a host of adjectives to describe our eating, not only the specifics of our diets but also the attentions we devote to food growth, preparation, and consumption. In the wake of such literary best-sellers as Barbara Kingsolver's *Animal, Vegetable, Miracle* (2008) and Michael Pollan's *The Omnivore's Dilemma* (2006), both individual artists and larger communities have turned to the production and consumption of food as issues of import. In October 2009, Ann Resnick curated *Omnivore's Delight,* an exhibition held at Project Gallery in Wichita, Kansas. Bringing together artists who address food in varied ways, Resnick framed the show as a celebration of America's renewed interest in local food, low-impact living, community gardening and good cooking (Resnick, 2009).

Many of the artists exhibiting in *Omnivore's Delight* hailed from the Midwest, America's heartland of food production. Perhaps fittingly, then, some addressed growth and manufacturing processes. In many of her photographs, Dana Fritz underscores the human desire to control and replicate nature

Museums & Social Issues, Volume 7, Number 1, Spring 2012, pp. 91–94.

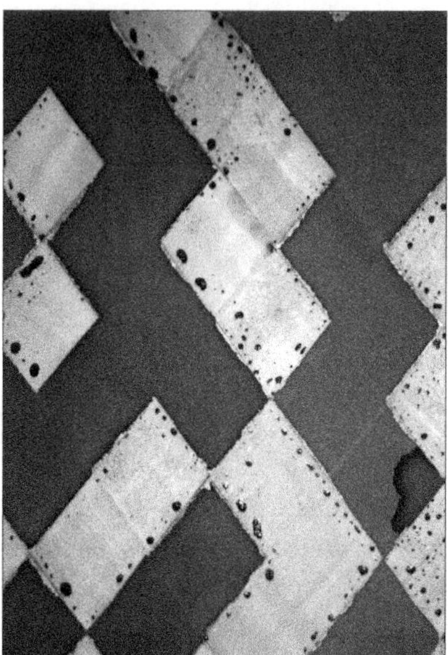

Kevin Mullins, detail of **BBW,** 2009. Local beet juice and beeswax on paper.

even through artificial means. In *Night Harvest: Tomatoes* and *Night Harvest: Haricots Verts* (both 2009), Fritz suggested the control impulses found among growers who harvest at night in the hopes of yielding the best possible produce. In *Twittervore* (2009), Mike Odom created a video mash-up of the countless images of food preparation and presentation found on social media sites. For this installation, Odom juxtaposed the video projection with United States map imagery, making reference to the geographies of food production.

Other contributors approached food from specific consumption references. In *Past, Repast* (2009), Resnick adorned a table as if for a ceremonial feast. Draping the table with delicately burnt paper reminiscent of lace cloth and topped with cast paraffin candles and candleholders, Resnick invited her viewers to contemplate the manner of their eating. How often do we take the time to honor and enjoy our food and those with whom we eat? Patrick Duegaw's *Breakfast with Elizabeth* (2000) offered an answer, monumentalizing in paint and sheetrock a daily, ordinary occurrence.

In some cases, food became the medium to deliver the message. Kevin Mullins used beeswax and beet juice to create a series of geometrically patterned works on paper. Emphasizing the importance of supporting area growers, Mullins identified both the beet juice and beeswax as local food-media. In *The Choad Parade* (2009), Kristin Beal-DeGrandmont transformed egg shells into phallic stacks of varied size and shape. My own series of screenprints, *The Food Landscape* (2007–2008), employed a variety of foods as inks. Chronicling the end of my breastfeeding journey and my youngest child's entry into solid foods, I kept a log of the foods my child ate each day during the 10 months of her gradual weaning. As I later created one print for each day of this journey, the natural dyes leached from those same foods became the inks for the prints themselves.

As an extension of the exhibition, *Omnivore's Delight* moved outside of the gallery walls with an outdoor community potluck dinner. Resnick invited community gardeners and activists, locavores, artists, and cooks to share dishes created from local food sources. Mike Odom recalled his locally sourced contributions: "home cured bacon, home cured pastrami, a salad of purple hull peas we grew in the community garden, some home canned okra pickles, and some home canned pickled watermelon rind." (Odom, 2009) Rather than positioning food production and consumption as a dilemma to be resolved, Resnick's exhibition and accompanying dinner embraced the food activism of artists and the Wichita community with celebratory zeal. Delightful, indeed.

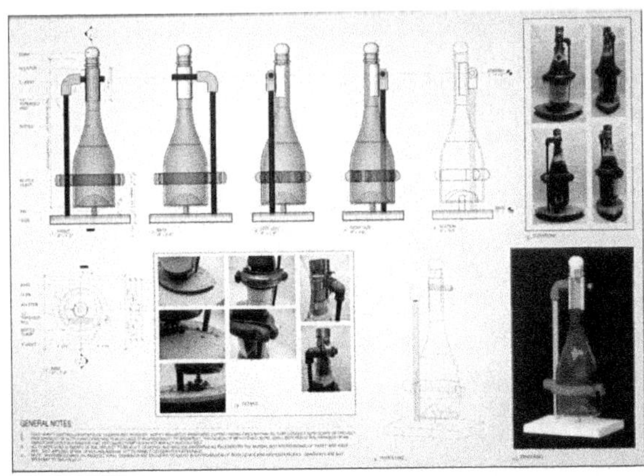

Elizabeth Stevenson, Indulge/ Abstain (Feast Days and Fast Days), 2009. Digital plot.

References

Kingsolver, B. (2008). *Animal, vegetable, miracle: A year of food life.* New York: Harper Perennial.

Odom, M. (2009). "A food show." www.art-commerce.blogspot.com/2009/10/food-show.html.

Pollan, M. (2006). *The omnivore's dilemma: A natural history of four meals.* New York: Penguin.

Resnick, A. (2009). "*Omnivore's Delight* Press Release." Email to the author, September 4, 2009.

Rachel Epp Buller (PhD) is Assistant Professor of Art at Bethel College in Kansas, an independent curator and artist, and regional coordinator of The Feminist Art Project. Her book *Reconciling Art and Mothering* was published by Ashgate in 2012.

Savoring Androscoggin County

Food, Performance and Community (Maine)

Myron M. Beasley

> *People ask me: Why do you write about food, and eating and drinking? Why don't you write about the struggle for power and security, and about love, the way others do?...The easiest answer is to say that, like most other humans, I am hungry.... There is a communion of more than bodies when bread is broken and wine drunk.*
>
> —M. F. K. Fisher (1954)

> *[T]he curator can have the power to manipulate any kind of situation, he or she should be able to invent the spaces . . . creating a special gallery, for instance or make an exhibition outside in the courtyard or some other place...making certain elements of that city or that community come together to discuss a particular issue.*
>
> —Mari-Carmen Ramirez (2001, p. 35)

Savoring Androscoggin County was a performative meal that took place in a vacant mill building in Lewiston, Maine. The project was a collaboration between Bates College and Museum L-A, both located in Androsocoggin County. The city of Lewiston has undergone several incarnations from an area that was a leading producer of textiles and shoes in the United States with an influx of French Canadians at the turn of the century, to its desolation with the closing of the mills sending labor abroad beginning in the late 1970s, to the recent influx of Somali immigrants and

Museums & Social Issues, Volume 7, Number 1, Spring 2012, pp. 95–100.

The memorial to the shoe workers who worked in the mill. *Photo courtesy of Phyllis Graber Jensen.*

the city's renewal efforts in the midst of the presence of the large vacant mill buildings as a constant reminder of the area's past. Museum L-A, which is housed in one of the mills, endeavors to document such shifts, to preserve local history, and to bring disparate communities together.

In 2007, the city of Lewiston was named an "All-American City" by the National Civic League. Despite the city's donning of the "All-American City" label, the issue of hunger continues to plague this local community and was brought to the foreground by Naomi Schalit's national award winning newspaper series, "For I Was Hungry" (2008). Despite Maine's ambitious and successful program of "selling and eating local," in which a high volume of locally grown produce remains in the state, the Maine farmer and the concept of the local farmer is on a steady decline. Given national concerns regarding food, an impetus for the *Savoring Androscoggin County* project was to seriously investigate food politics of the local community, seriously interrogating how issues of hunger, waste, production, as well as consumption are "performed" and made known.

The concept of the performative meal has been a mode that artists have used to call attention to political and social concerns. It is a theatrical performance, often highly themetized, where the mere presentation of food and food items attends to a variety of human senses. As Kirshenblatt-Gimblett (1999, p. 24) observes, "performance artists working on the line between art and life—denying the line, cross it, bringing art into life and life into art—are particularly attentive to the phenomenal, one might even say phenomenological, nature of food and the processes associated with it." *Savoring Androscoggin County* was a performance that revealed the interstitial space between food and performance and how such a space can contribute to the construction of creating and sustaining communities through eating together.

Twenty students from across the United States—with only one student representing Maine— enrolled in the Bates College course "Food, Performance and Community." The course description read:

> This interdisciplinary seminar examines the idea of cultural engagement through food. We will examine some of the meanings of food and eating across cultures, with particular attention to local community, particularly Androscoggin County. Considering performance ethnography as a lens by which we can grasp history, consumption, food desire and hunger both past and present in this locality. We will create a performative feast that reflects the culture of Androscoggin County.

The course was modeled after the WPA program "What America Eats," a federally funded unfinished program that employed famous American writers and artists and dispatched them across the United States to ascertain the status of food culture, sustainability, and hunger. The students were similarly "dispatched across" Androscoggin County to work with social workers, farmers, food pantries, restaurateurs, and other community members. After four weeks in the field, the students

Table of memories. *Photo courtesy of Phyllis Graber Jensen.*

returned with data (oral histories, transcribed interviews, statistical data, photographs, maps, and so forth) that were then translated into a performative meal.

The performance and the course highlighted creative uses of food and how food could tell the story of a place. The performance, which made use of the empty mill as the backdrop and the remains of what was left in the mill buildings as artifacts, accommodated 100 guests. It began with a memorial to the shoe workers—over 1,000 shoe molds were placed throughout an entire floor of the mill, interspersed with old machine parts and students posing as workers. While they ate from strategically placed trays of appetizers, the audience watched from afar and witnessed the silhouettes of the workers, the machines, and the shoes.

The next station was a series of five "peep rooms" which were constructed with Jacquard cards (punched cards used to control weaving on a loom) with students performing actions reflecting food production in the area inside the rooms. The long table of memories was a space were the audience members sat at a long narrow table with a one red hot dog (reflecting the traditional red dogs of the area) in front of each and were asked to share a food memory and engage with the stranger across from them. Nearby was the cotton installation—students wrapped in the barrels of raw cotton played with the audience that fed them goat cheese balls. The performance culminated in a large feast of items referencing the students' interviews and local traditional foodways.

To locate food as performance according to Kirshenblatt-Gimblett is "to perform… is to behave" as a conceptual point of convergence between food and performance. To perform in this sense is to "behave appropriately in relation to food at any point in its production, consumption or disposal" (1999, p. 2). The performative meal in the mill building foregrounds the complex web and possibilities of relationships between food and performance and food as community building. Jochnowitz (2001) reminds us that foodways is a set of cultural performances that assist in understanding the historical, economic, and religious practices of communities. "Foodways may be one part of a large and complicated set of cultural performances…telling insiders and outsiders who we are" (p. 56) and from whence we come.

From red hotdogs and Moxie soda, to a soup kitchen, to Somali samosas, to the French Canadian tradition of Tourtiere (meat pie), *Savoring Androscoggin County* provided a space where various aspects of the community (Franco-American, Somali, college students, museum staff, college staff members, farmers, restauranteurs) were brought together through eating. The food performance provided a space for people to discuss several sensitive political issues (hunger, racism, and immigration) that fester in the community.

Funding for this project was supported by grants from the Mellon Learning Associate Fund, Harward Center Grant for Public Engaged Academic Projects, Bates College Lectures Committee, and Museum L/A. The video of this performance can be viewed at: www.youtube.com/watch?v=5mVXEyUmY_s

References

Fisher, M.L.K. (1954). *The art of eating*. Cleveland: World Publishing.
For I Was Hungry. (2008, July). *Kennebec Journal*, A 16.
Jochnowitz, E. (2001). Edible activism. *Gastronomica, 2*, 56–63.
Kirshenblatt-Gimblett, B. (1999) Playing to the Senses: Food as a Performance Medium. *Performance Research, 4*, 1–30.
Ramirez, Mari-Carmen. (2001). Panel statements and discussion. In P. Maricola (Ed.), *Curating now: Imaginative Practice/Public Responsibility* (pp. 23–46). Philadelphia: Philadelphia Exhibitions Initiative.

Myron M. Beasley is Associate Professor of African American Studies and American Cultural Studies at Bates College, Lewiston, Maine. He is a critical ethnographer, curator, and performance artist. He is the 2010/11 recipient of an Andy Warhol Arts Writers Grant and a Whiting Foundation Fellowship for his work exploring gender performance among street food vendors of Jacmel and contemporary Haitian artists. Beasley is currently working on a book project on the topic of death and performance art in the African diaspora. He has curated projects in Haiti, Brazil, and Morocco, and his writing appears in journals such as *The Journal of Curatorial Studies, Text and Performance Quarterly*, and *Performance Research*.

A Sustainable Table

Living History (Maryland)

Lisa Hayes and Matt Mattingly

Much of the farmland that was once in the shadow of the nation's capital has, in recent years, been lost. With it has disappeared the sense of community that is so often tied to agriculture. Working to educate the public about agriculture's past, present, and future just 15 miles from Washington, DC, is the Accokeek Foundation at Piscataway Park. The Accokeek Foundation's National Colonial Farm is a living history museum that interprets ordinary life in colonial Maryland.

Food is a central theme in the work of the Accokeek Foundation at Piscataway Park. As we interpret agriculture's past, present, and future, we exhibit heirloom vegetables and traditional growing techniques; we are home to heritage livestock; and we grow organic produce to provide to local residents through a community supported agriculture program. But it is our Colonial Foodways program on the National Colonial Farm that provides visitors with the greatest understanding of how food connects each of us to the history and traditions of our ancestors.

Many living history museums offer "foodways" programs, which often focus on the food traditions appropriate to the museum's interpretive story. The National Colonial Farm interprets the life of a middling tobacco planter and his family, based on the recommendations of several noted scholars of 18th century Chesapeake history. Their study of more than 50 probate

Museums & Social Issues, Volume 7, Number 1, Spring 2012, pp. 101–104.

Matt Mattingly, Manager of the National Colonial Farm and the creative force behind the site's foodways program, leads a kitchen table conversation about 18th century Maryland food traditions.

inventories in Maryland's Charles and Prince George's counties from the last quarter of the 18th century revealed that such planters cooked with little more than a frying pan and a pot—important evidence that one-pot meals were a primary form of sustenance.

The foodways program at the National Colonial Farm began years ago as a way to use costumed volunteers to help interpret colonial history through the simple act of preparing a meal. But how could we inspire today's palate with ever-present and seemingly bland pottage, or flat yellow Johnny cakes? How could we reinvent the program to reflect the dynamic conversations that seem to be a matter of course at a site where a day at the office can include a buffet of freshly picked hot peppers, a lesson in harvesting a heritage breed chicken, or a debate about the most flavorful variety of heirloom tomatoes? How could we engage visitors and ourselves in an exploration of not just what we eat, but why?

Both agricultural and culinary traditions are rooted in the life of a community. For people in Southern Maryland, that life revolved for more than two centuries around growing tobacco. But agriculture has declined, and farms are giving way to residential developments inhabited by people who are new to the state and know little of the region's rich history. This loss of farmland represents far more than the transformation of a landscape from rural to urban; it marks the dissolution of a community and the creation of a sub-division culture.

With all of this in mind, we set out to create a foodways program that would provide a framework for engaging our visitors in a conversation about food, history, and community. We decided to combine the idea of a cooking show with the notion of a kitchen table conversation, and to focus the program on celebrating Maryland's rich culinary traditions and the ways in which these foods and traditions have changed over time. One program was called "Bristles and Feathers," a title drawn from the 18th century diary of Nicholas Cresswell, who lamented, "I have had either Bacon or Chickens every meal since I came into the Country. If I continue in this way I shall be grown over with Bristles or Feathers." *Where's the Beef (and or Venison)?!* focused on the staple meats of colonial America, as we demonstrated pickling beef, discussed preservation techniques used by Native Americans, and introduced our heritage breed cattle. But the most satisfying foodways program in 2011 was October's immersion in the secrets of Southern Maryland Stuffed Ham, a vernacular dish that is one of Maryland's oldest food traditions.

Matt Mattingly, manager of National Colonial Farm and the creative force behind the foodways program, comes from a family whose Southern Maryland roots go back to the 17th century. For Matt, stuffed ham is the mainstay of a holiday meal. His family's recipe was handed down to him by his mother, who received it from her mother, of whom it was said after she passed, "She could stuff a ham." Kale and cabbage are the principal actors in stuffed ham. Hot peppers, celery, mustard seed, and other "secrets" round out the cast of a dish that is lovingly described in Edna Ferber's novel *Showboat*: "Queenie had, for example, a way of stuffing a ham for baking. It was a fascinating process to behold, and one that took hours. Spices—bay, thyme, onion, clove, mustard, allspice, pepper—chopped and mixed and stirred together. A sharp-pointed knife plunged deep into the juicy ham. The incision stuffed with the spicy mixture. Another plunge with the knife. Another filling. Again and again and again until the great ham had grown to twice its size."

A couple who attended this program contacted us several days later to say they had procured a corned ham from the local butcher and were in the process of gathering the rest of the needed ingredients. Soon after, we received an email whose heading simply read, "WE DID IT!" They thanked us again and told us how happy they were that they were able to create a new tradition in their household.

On her popular cooking show "Lidia's Italy," chef Lidia Bastianich said, "A culture stays relevant and vibrant through its cuisine." Food brings people together. We are grateful that our quest to welcome people into the story of Maryland's history has led to old-timers and transplants gathering around our kitchen table to share their stories of food and tradition.

Lisa Hayes (PhD) is the President and CEO of the Accokeek Foundation, with more than 20 years of experience in arts administration, educational theater, oral history, and museums. She received her doctorate in American Studies from the State University of New York at Buffalo. Matt Mattingly is Manager of the National Colonial Farm and Historic Interpretation at the Accokeek Foundation. His extensive research on the 18th century tobacco culture of Southern Maryland continues to shape the foundation's educational and interpretive programs.

Eat Your Art Out

Artists Examine Our Relationship with Food (California)

Heather Richards Siddons and Alyssa Cordova

We do it three times a day with our hands and mouths in coordinated movement. Sometimes with careful planning and artistry; other times mindlessly and on the go; sometimes as a personal guilty pleasure, or in celebration with others: We consume food.

Food does not merely fulfill a biological need; it also ties cultures, regions, and generations to each other. Passed down over centuries, food is a type of storytelling; it traces migratory movements, evokes the immigrant experience, and underscores the cross-cultural marriage of people to place.

Food also connotes social status, oftentimes unabashedly proclaiming one's allegiance to country or class or, in a broader sense, taste. Historian Massimo Montanari argues, "Taste is a cultural product, not, in fact, subjective and incommunicable, but rather collective and eminently communicative. It is a cultural experience transmitted to us from birth" (Montanari, 2006, p. 62). In recent years, the idea of food and cooking as a cultural product has benefitted from a renewed focus, thanks in part to cable television cooking shows; increased public awareness of farming, consumption, and food politics; and the proliferation of impassioned food movements, such as *slow food*, pop-up restaurants, progressive dining, and gourmet food trucks.

Museums & Social Issues, Volume 7, Number 1, Spring 2012, pp. 105–107.

Entrance to "Acquired Taste" installation.
Photograph by Michael Quinn.

Acquired Taste: Food and the Art of Consumption, curated by Alyssa Cordova and Heather Richards Siddons, focused on our reciprocal relationship with food—what we consume, how we consume it, and how it consumes us. On view from October 29, 2011, through December 11, 2011, in the Lee & Nicholas Begovich Gallery at California State University, Fullerton, the exhibition explored the unrivalled importance of food in our daily lives and the transformative nature of this most primary of all human needs. The 13 artists of *Acquired Taste* represented a cross-section of contemporary approaches in a variety of media, including painting, installation, and sculpture. Sita Kuratomi Bhaumik's installations of curry and sugar alluded to identity, race, and class. Shannon Hayes Faseler investigated the temporal beauty of decaying food in the wake of a national disaster. Dustin Wayne Harris's *Cake Mixx* photographs offered a humorous, narrative take on relationships. Pamela Michelle Johnson's portraits of junk food reflected the excesses of Western culture, and Jennifer L. Knox inverted the authoritative stance of the author through the reappropriation of a cookbook. Timothy Berg and Rebekah Myers provoked the audience to consider how our consumption of goods is often greater

"Acquired Taste" opening reception, cooking demonstration. *Photograph by Kurt Simonson.*

than available resources. Mary Parisi's photographs depicted the alienating yet beautiful qualities found in food. Justin Perricone graphically depicted the litany of ingredients in a Hot Pocket as a subtle reflection on the commercial food industry. Victoria Reynolds's luscious meat paintings explored the duality of attraction and repulsion. Jennifer Rubell's participatory work used food as a vehicle for social commentary, interaction, and conversation. Stephen J. Shanabrook delivered a disquieting take on addiction through forms normally associated with comfort. Greg Stewart's work envisioned the future of agriculture and its potential effect on food supplies. Tattfoo Tan's *Nature Matching System* mural replicated colors found in nature so as to offer the viewer a methodology for choosing the foods we eat.

In the exhibition *Acquired Taste: Food and the Art of Consumption,* food is symbolic of the human condition in all of its messy and often complicated iterations. Food forms the basis of some of our earliest memories. It connects us to each other in conspicuous and imperceptible ways, binding us inextricably to our understanding of who we are, where we have come from, and where we long to be. After all, we are what we eat.

In conjunction with the exhibition, the opening reception for Acquired Taste *featured an appearance by community educator and master preserver Delilah Snell and cooking demonstrations and tastings by culinary expert and instructor Jonathan Dye. A full-color exhibition catalog is slated for publication in April 2012 and includes essays by freelance writer Nicole Caruth and art historian and blogger Megan Fizell, as well as original recipes by Jonathan Dye.*

Reference

Montanari, M. (2006). *Food is culture.* New York: Columbia University Press.

Alyssa Cordova is an MFA candidate in Exhibition Design and Museum Studies at California State University, Fullerton (CSUF). In 2010 she was selected as the CSUF Grand Central Art Center Graduate Fellow. She lives in Long Beach, California, with her husband and daughter. Heather Richards Siddons holds a BA in Art History from California State University, Long Beach and is a 2012 MFA candidate in Exhibition Design and Museum Studies at CSUF. She lives in Fullerton, California with her husband. In 2009, Cordova, Richards Siddons, and four other curator/artists founded Sixpack Projects, a six-person collective (www.sixpackprojects.com) that curates contemporary exhibitions throughout Southern California.

A Matter of Taste

Food, Faith, and Museums (California)

Carin Jacobs

Introduction

When I heard that *Museums & Social Issues* was assembling a volume on museums and food, I immediately felt compelled to submit something that would profile my professional activities at the nexus of these two worlds. As that tale alone might not provide sufficient fodder for an article, I decided to expand the story to explore what my three immediate spheres of work—museums, food, and faith—have in common. Perhaps this would help me to understand how, and why, I came to situate all three in a unique academic setting for the first time. As a caveat, I have no formal training in religious studies or theology. I came to the Graduate Theological Union (GTU) to work with the arts, and do not proclaim to teach the students about faith. What I have done is to provide "lens" classes that create new ways of examining faith. My lenses of choice have been museums and food. What do these have in common, and why was I drawn to both fields? First, they share the trait of interdisciplinarity. Second, they are both somewhat anthropological, and relate to the study of culture. What I will attempt to do here is to triangulate these three fields—museums, food, and faith—to examine the connective tissue between them and the ways in which they overlap.

Museums & Social Issues, Volume 7, Number 1, Spring 2012, pp. 109–113.

What Does Food Have To Do with Faith?

I could begin with the notion of service: on the one hand, the tableside theater with wait staff; on the other hand, the worship event in a sacred space. My course *Flavors of Faith* ranges from taboos and prohibitions to "Liquid Courage," (exploring the ritual aspects of both wine and tea), to an exploration of food communities and food ministry, Community Supported Agriculture (CSA) farmer's markets, monasteries and food production, and interfaith restaurants as community catalysts. The course concludes with an exploration of gendered images of women and food, and the notion of "performing" food, from the theater of restaurant culture to contemporary artists who use food as a medium for their work. For final projects, students have chosen topics as disparate as the canning practices of Mormons, the importance of food and faith to the mentally ill, and wine as religion in the Napa Valley.

What Do Museums (and Art) Have To Do with Food?

I could say it's all a matter of taste: on the one hand, subjective judgment, and on the other, an objective use of the bodily senses to make meaning. Just as we hear of high art and low art, Kant dismisses taste, smell, and touch as the "lower senses" while privileging vision and hearing. He goes on to say that knowledge produced through the sense of taste is immediate and immersive, while visual knowledge requires separation. It is impossible to see something contiguous to the eye; one must move away. These sensory politics play out in the aesthetics of food and the duality of taste in culinary and museum settings.

The aesthetics of food—from the cover of *Bon Appetit*, to the art of sushi, to a still life in the making—are integral to visual culture in both domestic and public settings. Wayne Thiebaud's cover illustrations from the annual food issues of *The New Yorker* have become iconic. Food has permeated the media as well. On the big screen, *Julie and Julia* (2009) and *Ratatouille* (2007) explore foodways in both human and cartoon universes. On television, we see demonstration shows, competition shows, and inspirational shows, all centered around food. Monica Mak's (2006) surprising article "The Pixel Chef: PBS Television Cooking Shows and Sensorial Utopias" introduces the idea of television as an "anaesthetic medium" that deadens the senses (p. 258). How, then, are we to experience these shows in which sensory engagement is critical? We must rely on visual and aural cues, and through a leap of faith (another triangulation) vicariously smell, touch, and taste the food being presented. We must, it seems, suspend our disbelief to enjoy the illusion of a complete sensory experience.

What Does Faith Have To Do with Museums?

My students and I have spent a good deal of time considering whether the museum can be, or should be, a sacred space. I think we agree that the museum is a safe place for the collision of perspectives, be they political, intellectual, or spiritual. Museums have also been said to inspire trust and to provoke conversation. What better site, then, might there be for catalyzing interfaith dialogue, appreciation, and understanding? David Carr (2006) states, "By definition, every religious object in a secular museum is reduced in power by its separation from its original contexts" (p. 77). This begs the question: Is the spirit(uality) in the object, the user, or the ritual? One could ask the same of "soul" food. Is the soul in the food, the preparer, or the consumer?

The objects and images in museums can make the invisible visible, giving corporeal form to ideas and beliefs. They can also illustrate the intimacy of creation and introduce creativity as a spiritual practice. Perhaps museums can also serve to mediate the debate between science and religion, as they are at once rational and expressive entities. As a nexus of analysis and intuition, the museum sits at the juncture of two worlds.

I have a book on my desk whose provocative title often sparks conversation. Ena Giurescu Heller's *Reluctant Partners: Art and Religion in Dialogue* profiles the historic, and often very public, tensions between these two worlds. However, as we study the language used in both fields—creation...creator...creativity—perhaps these disciplines are not as far apart as Heller's title suggests. How are the museums and galleries on faith-based campuses, such as the Doug Adams Gallery at GTU, situated to blur these boundaries? How much overlap is there between museum, worship space, and classroom? How permeable are these definitions?

Conclusion (a Sense of Place)

The San Francisco Bay area is a mecca for artisan food, organic food, food philosophy, and food communities. Chez Panisse, a pioneering organization in the culinary world, is located mere blocks from the GTU in Berkeley. The Ferry Building Public Market in San Francisco has become one of the largest in the nation. Locally sourced produce and meats share prime real estate with freshly baked breads and small batch wines and spirits, as farmers and other food producers and purveyors proudly display their wares. In the midst of this culinary/cultural landscape, restaurants and museums have established themselves as gathering places, essential to their communities, reflecting what sociologist Ray Oldenburg termed "third place" (in contrast to the first and second places of home and work). He argues that bars, coffee shops, general stores, and churches are all sites of social activity—where adults voluntarily go to participate in civil society. They triangulate the material, behavioral, and cognitive aspects of culture. This balance will continue to drive my work at GTU, in the classroom and in the gallery, with museums, food, and faith each bringing something to the table.

References

Carr, D. (2006). *A place not a place: Reflection and possibility in museums and libraries*. Lanham, Maryland: Altamira Press.

Mak, M. (2006). The pixel chef: PBS television cooking shows and sensorial utopias. In E. A. Madden & M. L. Finch (Eds.), *Eating in Eden Food & American utopias* (p. 258). Lincoln: University of Nebraska Press.

Carin Jacobs, Director of the Center for the Arts, Religion and Education and the Doug Adams Gallery at the Graduate Theological Union in Berkeley, California, is an educator, arts administrator, and scholar of museum studies. Her work focuses on museum literacy and the integration of museums in college teaching, and she has presented workshops around the country and published a number of articles about museums and higher education.

Tapas from Across and Outside the United States

Museums, Food, and Art

(California)

Lisa A. Silagyi

Food brings people together. Food defines, redefines, and reinforces cultures. Food is nourishment, a part of our daily lives for survival. Food provides us with an appreciation of simple pleasures, as well as decadent indulgences.

The slow food movement has grown exponentially in recent years. Although originating in Italy, the idea of buying locally and organically attempts to counter the American culture's loss of understanding about where our food comes from and how it is prepared. The slow food movement is in direct response to fast foods, processed foods, and the loss of the culinary art, tradition, and nutrition that come with enjoying the freshest produce and meats available.

Cooking is an art. Taking time to slow down and appreciate the subtleties and nuances of what we eat is a habit worth cultivating. Visiting an art museum and reflecting on a work of art provides a similar kind of experience. They share in common the creative impulse, production, reflection, and a heightening of our senses to the everyday world. Art and food have been intertwined from the beginning. Images of beer and bread adorn the walls of Egyptian tombs in the form of banquet feasts for the ancient pharaohs; dewy fruits, wine, and wild game are richly captured in 17th century Dutch still life paintings; and colorful and succulent

Museums & Social Issues, Volume 7, Number 1, Spring 2012, pp. 115–119.

Instructor Jeff Venier with students during a Jr. Chef class at the Center for Living Peace. *Photo courtesy of the Center for Living Peace.*

cakes in diner windows are composed in thickly applied paint in the 20th century work of artist Wayne Thiebaud.

The Orange County Museum of Art (OCMA) in Newport Beach, California, is recognized as one of the finest mid-sized museums in America dedicated to the display of modern and contemporary art. The museum is situated in Southern California, one of the most outstanding climates in the world for food production.

In 2010, OCMA began a partnership with the Center for Living Peace (CLP), a local non-profit organization in Irvine, California. The Center acts as a community resource where people of all ages can "connect to self and their spirit, to others, and to the world." Their vision is to "inspire inner peace and the collective expression of living peacefully." The museum offers classes at the CLP related to art, art making, and the notion of living peace.

ARTful Eating

Healthy eating and good nutrition were the emphasis of a series of classes, titled *ARTful Eating*. One of the museum's teaching artists, also an amateur chef, farmer, and wine connoisseur, became the link between contemporary art and the culinary world. Students would visit a farmer's market in the parking lot where the center is located, talk to vendors, and purchase food that would later be the subject of drawing activities. Finally, the hungry group would prepare a series of dishes and sit down to eat together.

As part of this partnership, the museum created programming around the topics of art and food. A workshop titled *A Taste of California Food and Wine* was designed in conjunction with an exhibition at OCMA, *State of Mind: New California Art Circa 1970.* Co-curated by Karen Moss and Constance Lewallen, *State of Mind* is an investigation of the conceptual practices of over 50 artists creating work in the late 60s and early 70s in California. The exhibition showcases young artists of the period experimenting with performance art, new technologies such as video and sound art, street art, and installation works that push to redefine the meaning of art. Artists were responding to the tumultuous time, expressing concerns about the environment, racism, sexism, and the Vietnam War.

The class brought together the celebration of California art history that is currently occurring throughout California led by the J. Paul Getty museum's "Pacific Standard Time (PST)" initiative, and the celebration of all of the delicious food and wine grown locally in the Golden State.

In addition to providing students with a sampling of California wines, cheeses, and vegetable dishes, images of works from the exhibition were projected. As students sampled and delighted in learning about where to buy and how to prepare locally grown foods, they also deconstructed the images they saw from the exhibition. Questions of place, the environment, experimentation, and what it means to be "Californian" were topics of discussion. Gaining a heightened appreciation and sensitivity to the environment around us through artful living is indeed a skill worth cultivating.

Description of Classes

ARTful Eating

Everyday life has sped up to such an extent that most of us barely think about what we eat or who produced it. But what if we changed our approach; thought about dinner ahead of time, met the person who grew our vegetables, and truly appreciated the food we share around the table with our loved ones? This class celebrates the summer season and practices the art of good health. As a group, we will visit the Irvine Farmer's Market, meet local vendors, and prepare delicious composed salads together. We'll use these goodies as a source of inspiration for a class still life to draw from. Student drawings will be mounted with the cool summer recipes as a memento for you.

This class is in conjunction with the Orange County Museum of Art's 2010 California Biennial.

A Taste of California Food and Wine

Often our lives are so busy that we forget to practice gratitude for our amazing California climate, which produces some of the best wines and produce in the world. Join teaching artist Jeff Venier for a celebratory evening of locally-grown foods and wines that we will sample together. Get to know new people in your community and learn why it's important to buy locally!

This class is in conjunction with the Orange County Museum of Art's State of Mind: New California Art Circa 1970 exhibition, on view through January 22, 2012.

Reference

The Center for Living Peace. (2010). About us: Our vision and mission. Retrieved February 1, 2012, from www.goodhappens.org

Lisa Silagyi is the Director of Education and Public Programs at the Orange County Museum of Art in Newport Beach, California. She was the recipient of the 2011 Pacific Region Art Museum Educator of the Year award of the National Art Education Association.

Eating Art, Sharing Food, Writing History

(Cyprus)

Christina Vatsella

Having food as a point of departure, Cypriot visual artist Lia Lapithi develops a multifarious project evoking recent political history. The traumatic experience of the 1974 war in Cyprus is being unfolded in a multi-layer work that focuses on the way history is being written, experienced, and transmitted via the culinary culture.

During this three-year long project, two major exhibitions were organized, the first in Nicosia (Cyprus) and the second in Athens. Each show was conceived as a unified installation comprising interrelated artworks. The museum galleries were thus transformed into large dining rooms where people could literally eat artworks or watch gastronomy related videos on the screens.

A Symposium: The Exhibition in Cyprus

The exhibition *A Symposium* is conceived by the artist as an invitation to a traditional Greek feast, encouraging the viewer to construct his/her own personal conceptual route via images, tastes, and fragrances.

A table set in anticipation of the diners dominates the space. The dinnerware set predisposes us to the notion that Lapithis's main menu is modern political history. Each of the plates is painted with a mountain peak of Pentadaktylos, the occupied

Museums & Social Issues, Volume 7, Number 1, Spring 2012, pp. 121–124.

mountain range, accompanied by the slogan "I don't forget," a phrase that has become a symbol for Greek Cypriots, condensing contemporary Cyprus history.

The most impressive work of the exhibition is a 10-meter white chocolate sculpture in the shape of Pentadaktylos's 19 peaks. The viewer is called upon to cut a piece of the artwork and to eat it. Within the framework of an exhibition structured around the subject of taste, encouraging the viewer to eat a piece of the artwork seems quite natural. At the same time, on a symbolic level, "eating" means appropriating something in a primordial way. Viewers are invited to taste Pentadaktylos, literally endorsing its effigy, while at the same time they are free to journey through their personal memories on its 19 legendary mountain peaks.

Let's Talk About Peace Over Dinner: A Performance and an Exhibition

The starting point of this project is a formal dinner in the form of a performance. Artist Lia Lapithi constructs the event methodically, creating a setting to which she assiduously applies a web of constant references to the theme of peace.

The artist receives her guests to a formal and exceptionally elegant banquet set. The 19 dinner guests, as many as the peaks of the Pendadaktylos Range, come from various countries. Each detail of the setting created by Lapithi renders visually the theme of the dinner. The table is adorned with arrangements based on olive branches, while the handmade china is decorated with the mountain peaks of Pendadaktylos and with the phrase

Pendadaktylos Range, white chocolate sculpture by Lia Lapithi, 2010.

"I do not forget" being continuously repeated as the main motif and point of reference.

The dinner menu, full of symbolism, provides both literal and metaphorical food for thought, since it relates a story. The main course is made of a pigeon, the world symbol for peace, stuffed with a lotus flower, the fruit of oblivion. The dessert is a sweet of olives served on a layer of lemon sorbet, leaving a bitter-sweet flavour at the end of the dinner, a mixed feeling of euphoria and bitterness, rendering palatably the sense of life that goes on, while there is a wound in the background, an unresolved issue that cannot be forgotten. In order to prompt digestion, the artist proposes two beverages, squeezing into two cups the turbulent history of the country and the main players. The Cypriot or Greek or Turkish or Byzantine coffee makes the first choice an interminable quest for its national identity or simply a constant denial of its very history. Alternatively, the guests may choose tea made of olive leaves, an original beverage and innovative result of colonial fermentation.

The performance that took place in Cyprus provided the raw material for the creation of audiovisual installations. For the audio installation, the decorated table is transposed in its entirety and laid again at the galleries of the House of Cyprus in Athens. Through a system of multiple loudspeakers, the conversations of the guests fill the space, thus emphasizing their physical absence. Lapithi reconstitutes the setting of the original event, creating a work suspended between here and there, now and then, presence and absence. On a second level, the laid table without people, haunted by the voices of its absent guests, cannot but refer us to

Copyright the artist.

their houses, which were violently abandoned following the invasion of 1974, to be inhabited by others.

On the opposite side—of the room but of memory at the same time—the artist gives a representation in the form of a video installation. The three screenings that make up the basic triptych are combined, constituting a single image, the product of frontal shots of the dinner from three fixed cameras. It is a comprehensive recording that represents the event and transposes it visually to another space.

Opposite the triptych, Lapithi projects another video from the camera that was located above the guests and exclusively filmed the table. Nineteen pairs of hands, cut off from the rest of the body, interact with the plates and the glasses that alternate continuously, inviting the spectators to concentrate on the act itself. It is a different picture coming from a supplementary visual angle. The spectator is invited to mentally compose the diverse images so as to have the full visual text.

The representation of the event by Lapithi reproduces the mechanisms of memory. Every remembrance has a fragmented character since the picture sometimes fades, leaving only the sound and sometimes returns as a whole; at other times it is the product of concatenations that are prompted by specific objects. Even if someone tries consciously *not to forget,* the memory is mutated, gradually losing its initial tension but always remaining alive in one form or another. Even if one *does not forget,* one ends up reconciling oneself with the situation and lives in peace. And the dinner, ultimately, marks this inner truce.

Christina Vatsella is a PhD candidate in History of Art at the Université Paris Sorbonne—Paris IV. Her research focuses on the history of new media art, and her PhD subject is the question of space in the video installation. She is currently teaching History of Art and the New Media at the Université Paris-Est Marne-la-Vallée.

Book Review

Maman's Homesick Pie: A Persian Heart in an American Kitchen

By Donia Bijan

250 pages. Algonquin Books of Chapel Hill. 2011. PSBN 978-1-56512-957-3

Reviewed by Anita Verna Crofts

"The kitchen is my harbor": food and identity in exile.

Donia Bijan's sparkling memoir, *Maman's Homesick Pie: A Persian Heart in an American Kitchen,* is a nested love story of recipes, family, identity, and memory. An Iranian exile for over 30 years, Bijan writes "through the prism of food," a language she is deeply familiar with as a trained chef.

Bijan is a gifted storyteller. She holds readers spellbound as she carefully reveals her family history, paced appropriately like a fine meal. The coda to each chapter is two recipes that trace the edible arc of Bijan's personal narrative: Iranian childhood, American exile and resettlement in California, French culinary training, restaurant mastery and acclaim. One does not just read the recipes for cardamom tea, duck à l'orange, or rose petal ice cream, one is immersed in the stories that form the meaning behind the recipes. The greater meaning serves as a form of national preservation.

For it is in their meaning that recipes provide ballast to those forced to reinvent themselves, as exiles must. The life of an exile is one of profound disorientation. Bijan describes the summer of 1978 and her family's arrival for a vacation in Spain with "little more than beachwear, paperback books, and a backgammon set."

She was not to see Tehran again.

Museums & Social Issues, Volume 6, Number 2, Fall 2011, pp. 125–128.

Think about the last time you packed a suitcase and went through the mental checklist before departing your home: oven turned off, mail held, and lights on timers. Now imagine you never step foot in your home again, your new life built off the impermanence of a suitcase. It is no wonder that foodways become a powerful tether amidst such disorientation.

Bijan turns sixteen on Spanish soil, suspended in limbo with events still unstable in Iran and the future deeply uncertain. With her parent's blessing she leaves Europe for the midwestern United States to enroll her junior year in a private high school. As she navigates the complex social norms of teenagers, she finds customs around food and households to also be downright mystifying. "What struck me is how long you could be in someone's home before anyone offered you a glass of water (we were taught never to ask for anything). In an Iranian home, you are fed fifteen times before the mud on your shoes dries."

The negative perception Bijan encounters of her homeland in the United States of the 1970s further complicates the life of an Iranian exile. She adjusts her language accordingly. "*Persian* quickly replaced *Iranian*. Where *Iran* was dark and threatening, *Persia* recalled glory, carpets, and cats." This is made visible even in the title of her book. Sadly, a 21st century Iranian exile in the United States would be faced with equal, if not more wildly exaggerated, misconceptions of their native land.

At the heart of this book is Bijan's mother, whose death we mourn from the opening sentence. The cold reality of her mother's passing is juxtaposed by the remaining 249 pages which bring her personality to life in vivid detail: a London-trained Iranian midwife, "who spoke the Queen's English, listened to classical music turned up very loud on her hi-fi, smoked Winston cigarettes, kept a bust of Beethoven on her dresser, and carried a British driver's license in her purse." It's no wonder a young Dr. Bijan, "terribly handsome with bright blue eyes," falls hard and pursues her hand in marriage "within days" of meeting this captivating creature.

All marriages face tests, but the stress of exile and forced relocation must rank as one of the most challenging experiences any kinship unit must bear. Bijan's father is the one most haunted by exile in the United States, as he is forced to part with a flourishing medical career running a hospital that bears his name (with a penthouse apartment on the top floor of the hospital serving as the Bijan home). "He lamented the loss of his hospital as one would regret abandoning a relative in desperate times," writes Bijan.

By contrast, Bijan's mother, who served in the Iranian parliament as an outspoken feminist in the early 70s, accepts the cross-cultural challenges she faces in her adopted homeland with gusto—starting with food. "My mother cooked because it made her happy," write Bijan, "and when you sat at her table you shared her happiness." That joy and natural curiosity allow Bijan's mother to experiment with new recipes (apple pie, coleslaw, macaroni and cheese) while still cleaving to traditional Persian fare and relishing the local bounty that acts as a keen reminder of Tehran. "*Oh, look! Look! They have persimmons here,*" Bijan recalls the two of them thinking from an early walk in their suburban Bay Area neighborhood.

The book chapters skillfully glide between Bijan's acculturation to life in the United States, the tug of recollections that place her in Iran as a child, and her eventual culinary training at the Cordon Bleu in France ("France had given me a lasting parting gift: to leave a place with longing in your heart to return"), which culminates with her success as a chef back in California. Bijan's mother is her greatest champion each step of the way, in contrast to her father, who sees the pursuit of a career in cookery as an unforgivable choice. Dreadfully pedestrian.

And here in the story lies a bitterness: despite his unabashed love and appreciation for all things edible—this was a man who traveled with "an assortment of knives, corkscrews, can openers, salt and pepper mills, minibottles of mustard, olive oil, scotch, and vodka, and occasionally caviar"—Bijan's father cannot accept her life's calling. Bijan's mother may tend the hearth that makes the Bijan home, but her father contributes his own passion for fresh ingredients to his daughter, despite his misgivings of her career choice.

Bijan has a demonstrated talent when she picks up her knives in a kitchen, and her book provides rich insight into the rigors and sacrifices involved in pursuing a culinary degree and stewarding high-end restaurants. When she swaps plated meals for prose, Bijan brings the same care and creativity to the work of transforming words that lack inspiration on their own into memorable combinations. Many of her passages are feasts for the senses.

During an interview in 2011, Bijan explained that while the perception of exiles is one of untethered "betwixt and between," food can be a reassuring constant. "The kitchen is my harbor," she said.

When reading *Maman's Homesick Pie,* one cannot help but experience the literary equivalent of scraping up a chair around a well-used kitchen table and soaking up stories with no concept of the passage of time. Teacups will be refilled and dusk will eventually arrive. Readers are fortunate to let down their anchors in Bijan's safe harbor.

Anita Verna Crofts is on the faculty of the Department of Communication at the University of Washington and serves as the Associate Director for the Master of Communication in Digital Media Program. Her writings on food have been published widely, with a particular emphasis on the preservation of foodways in post-conflict societies as a means of preserving community identity.

Book Review

Everlasting Meal: Cooking with Economy and Grace

By Tamar Adler; Foreword by Alice Waters.
Simon & Schuster, Inc., New York. 2011. ISBN 978-1-4391-8187-4/ ISBN 978-1-4391-8189-8 (ebook)

Reviewed by Beck Tench

The first thing Tamar Adler tells you to do in *An Everlasting Meal: Cooking with Economy and Grace* is to boil a pot of water. She says that if you plan to cook, you'll likely need it anyway.

This simple instruction—to start cooking before you even know what you'll make—has profoundly changed the way I purchase, prepare, store, and eat food. The broccoli that goes into that pot of water will not just feed me today. The leftover stock, uneaten bits, and raw stems will be the start of another meal, some part of which will continue onto the next and so on.

Michael Pollan encourages us to "eat food. Not too much. Mostly plants." Adler shows us how. Through prose as tight as it is graceful, she persuades us to take our farmers' market finds and leave them on the table until they're cooked, lest they be forgotten in our refrigerators. She teaches us to roast, boil, braise, and sauté them into basics that can be grabbed throughout the week to make any number of meals and snacks. A butternut squash roasted on Sunday may become a soup on Monday, a sandwich filling on Tuesday, a frittata on Wednesday, and a warm winter salad on Thursday. With only four pieces left on Friday, it could be a key player in an omelet or curry dish.

She requires us to reuse carrot tops and onion tops, stems from greens and herbs, stale bread, water from our boiled vegetables and cooked beans, bones, and lemon peels. She insists

Museums & Social Issues, Volume 6, Number 2, Fall 2011, pp. 129–131.

Beck Tench's Winter Salad with Breadcrumbs. *Courtesy of author.*

our mistakes, too, warrant saving—the burnt, the over salted, the well done—for they can often be reinterpreted after the smoke, and our disappointment, has cleared.

Adler overrules rock star chefs who encourage a consumerist, complex, and gimmicky view of cooking and reminds us what a worthy thing it is to be a confident and creative home cook. Never is her strategy for the book clearer to me than when she quotes Antoine de Saint-Exupéry in the beginning of Chapter 12, "If you want to build a ship, don't drum up people to collect wood, and don't assign them tasks and work, but rather teach them to long for the endless immensity of the sea." If you want to create home cooks, don't give people recipes to mindlessly follow or intimidate them with culinary magic, but rather teach them to long for the making and eating of real food.

It then seems purposeful that her narrative outshines her recipes, which she peppers throughout, punctuating points made. I've found myself more often revisiting the paragraphs, looking for a mention of storing parsley or marinating onions so that I can create my own concoctions. Still, the recipes play an important part, putting practice within reach. In Adler's tradition, I shall do the same and end this review with one I created on my own, since boiling that first pot of water.

Winter Salad with Breadcrumbs

Recipe

- Ends of any bread that is not yet moldy.
- An assortment of leftover roasted vegetables.
- Parmigiano-Reggiano
- Olive Oil

To make breadcrumbs: Cut or tear crust-less bread into small pieces and pulse in food processor until desired size. Give a generous dousing of very good olive oil and spread out on a baking sheet. Put into a 400°F oven for 5-10 minutes, turning once or twice. Remove from baking sheet at once so they do not continue to bake. Store any leftovers in a jar in the fridge and use on soft things to add dimension and texture.

To make salad: Take leftover roasted vegetables (I recommend roasted broccoli, butternut squash and cabbage) out of the fridge and bring to room temperature on the counter (or if cooking something else, steal heat from it by placing the jars nearby). Once the chill is gone, mix a handful of each into a bowl and toss with a generous dousing of olive oil and breadcrumbs. Portion into bowls and top with grated cheese.

Beck Tench is a simplifier, illustrator, story-teller and technologist. She is Director for Innovation and Digital Engagement at the Museum of Life and Science in Durham, North Carolina, where she studies and experiments with how visitors and staff use technology to experience risk-taking, community-making, and science in their daily lives.

Program Review

Historic but not History

Sustainable Food Initiatives at Jane Addams Hull-House Museum, Chicago

Reviewed by Lisa Roberts

Hull-House was founded in Chicago in the late 19th century by the great social reformers Jane Addams and Ellen Gates Starr to offer arts and literary education to their less fortunate neighbors—mostly immigrants, many desperately poor. It became a place where people with widely diverse backgrounds could come together to learn English, reading, and a host of other practical skills needed to adjust to life in a new country. Over time, the settlement house expanded, adding services to support the social and educational needs of the community including childcare, vocational classes, and a public kitchen and bath, as well as cultural offerings like art, music, and theater—things to nurture both body and soul. Hull-House also became a place where reformers could meet and debate ways to bring about social change to secure the rights of laborers, women, children, and other unprotected groups.

While many of these activities have been memorialized in the museum now housed there, some remain vibrant programs refashioned to meet the needs of today. The Hull-House Museum may be a historic house, but its commitment to social reform is no artifact of the past. Here, history informs the present, well demonstrated by one of the museum's main focus areas: food. The availability of good, healthy food for every citizen is an issue that has never gone away. In Jane Addams's day, food justice was about providing safe milk for babies, teaching immigrants to cook using unfamiliar ingredients, and feeding the hungry. Today's food activists continue to fight the problem of hunger, but they are

Museums & Social Issues, Volume 6, Number 2, Fall 2011, pp. 132–136.

also concerned with promoting sustainable growing practices, eliminating food deserts, and reducing childhood obesity. Issues like these are the driving force behind five related programs that make up the Hull-House "Kitchen" today.

Rethinking Soup

One of two buildings that remain from the original Hull-House complex is the residents' dining hall where social reformers like Upton Sinclair, Ida B. Wells, and Gertrude Stein met to eat, share ideas, and conspire to change the world. Today the room is the site of a weekly modern day soup kitchen where people from all social strata come together around long communal tables to discuss pressing issues related to food justice. Guest chefs provide delicious, healthy (free) soup and bread; and invited speakers—activists, farmers, doctors, economists, artists, restauranteurs—lead a conversation each week about their research, projects, and ideas.

The kitchen, as a result, nurtures not just the physical body but the social body as well, by creating a space for community to gather, exchange ideas, and plot solutions. Of course, it also opens the proverbial can of worms, as the issues discussed have widespread implications for the entire system of food production and consumption, including that in which the kitchen itself is engaged. The Hull-House Museum walks its own talk, however, and has developed related programming that serves as a demonstration of responsible practice while supporting its own operations.

Heirloom Farm

One of the main issues around food access today has to do with its source and quality. "Sustainable" production has become the watchword for food activists concerned about the harmful practices of large-scale, profit-making agribusinesses where chemical treatments, genetically modified strains, poor labor practices, and vast distribution networks cause incalculable damage to the health of both people and the environment.

A half-acre urban farm outside of Hull-House offers a public demonstration of one alternative: small-scale, organic, local production. Visitors and volunteers are able to learn first-hand what it means to grow food sustainably and successfully. Several tons of fruits and vegetables are harvested from the site each season and are either used in the weekly soup, distributed to local community kitchens, or canned and preserved for later use.

The farm serves another purpose as well. By growing a wide variety of heirloom crops, it affirms—both literally and metaphorically—the value of diverse forms of food. From an ecological standpoint, crop variety offers greater natural resistance to the effects of pests and disease that can easily attack a monoculture. From a cultural standpoint, it reinforces the value of diverse traditions, identities, and stories associated with, for example, the Chinese napa cabbage or the Purple Cherokee tomato. The need for biological diversity, then, becomes an expression of the value of cultural diversity.

Heirloom Seed Library

Growing heirloom crops requires planting heirloom seeds, and the Seed Library was developed to address this need at a very local level. The program operates much as a library does: patrons use a Seed Library Card to check out any of a wide variety of regionally adapted seeds to plant in their gardens. Throughout the growing season, they collect the seeds from their harvested crops to return to the library.

The benefits of this program are many. It is a way to get many more varieties of seeds—especially those well suited to local growing conditions—into the hands of gardeners than might ordinarily be available at the average nursery. It is a way of conserving the remaining diversity of the planet's seed stock. And it is a way of sharing the extraordinary histories and stories behind particular varieties. For example, how many people know that the Trail of Tears bean was so named because the Cherokees subsisted on them on the infamous journey of the same name. The Seed Library is not a metaphor. Seeds contain a record of our past, and as long as they are cultivated, each generation will sow new stories about their growth and use.

Preserving Peace

Food access is also a temporal issue: how does one source local produce outside of the growing season—especially in climates where the land goes dormant for several months? Our forebears knew the answer; before the days of corner grocers and food distribution networks, canning and preserving excess produce was an essential kitchen activity. While no longer widely practiced, food preservation is a highly sustainable way of ensuring that local produce is available year round. The Hull-House Museum is doing its part to revive the tradition by offering classes and a free, downloadable guide to canning, preserving, and pickling food. Here, too, the museum practices what it preaches, preserving food from its own farm and selling it year round.

More than food is being preserved here, however. The museum is also preserving a long tradition of home economics practiced by trailblazing women for whom other professional opportunities were denied. The Hull-House Museum honors these women by featuring a key figure on each of the labels of its own preserved goods. Their stories are thus saved and passed on by means of the very methods that they pioneered and that are being re-valued today.

Hungry for Art

Finally, a somewhat different take on food: as a means of nourishing creativity. One of the major thrusts of the original Hull-House reformers was the provision of art and culture to feed the spirit. They felt that the spiritual self was every bit as important as the physical self for individuals to fully realize their potential as citizens and human beings. Hull-House was the site of Chicago's first public art gallery, founded so that people could contemplate beauty; and it also offered classes in music, painting, pottery, and more.

Hungry for Art follows this tradition but with its own, vegetative twist. The program takes food as the inspiration for creative expression, showcasing the results in a kind of communal art project. Visitors are invited to take one of the heirloom vegetables grown on the urban farm and create something with it—a dish, an instrument, a sculpture, anything the "radical imagination" may come up with. The program is a contemporary take on Hull-House's commitment to art-making as a way to create a common culture made up of unique differences.

Summary

Jane Addams believed that good health and nutrition are key to a just, peaceful, democratic society. Her sentiments still hold true, and on multiple levels. Clearly physical health is essential for individuals to function at their best. But social health is just as important, and food access is a concern for everyone who eats, no matter their background, no matter the era. The Hull-House Museum today continues to uphold these ideals along with Addams's vision and values of social justice for all. This is a "living history" museum redefined—re-enacting a past by adapting it to the needs and conditions of the present.

Lisa Roberts is an independent consultant for gardens, museums, parks, and other public spaces.